Praise for *Marketing Artificial Intelligence*

"For any marketer exploring the power of data and AI to create better outcomes for their customers and their business, *Marketing Artificial Intelligence* is an essential primer. This book lucidly explores a multitude of relevant use cases with examples, vendors to watch, and questions to reflect on. Best of all, the authors do a remarkable job of unpacking the possibilities for the reader, without drifting into technical complexity."
—Sheldon Monteiro, Chief Product Officer, Publicis Sapient

"When it comes to Marketing AI, Roetzer is one of the best at simplifying the complex—and in an easy and straightforward way everyone can understand. *Marketing Artificial Intelligence* is a must-read to understand how AI is evolving and transforming the discipline of marketing. It's what you need to know to stay ahead of the curve and deliver experiences that engage and wow consumers."
—Christi Olson, Head of Paid Search, Microsoft

"Today no business can succeed without a digital presence, and in the very near future no brand will succeed without AI. Roetzer and Kaput have done a masterful job with this book by giving you the roadmap of AI's impacts and how you can leverage them for a more successful future."
—Mathew Sweezey, Author of *The Context Marketing Revolution* (HBR) and Cofounder Salesforce Web3 Studio

"Tapping their deep expertise in the marketing applications of machine learning, Paul and Mike have written a masterful handbook for marketers looking to understand what AI/ML can actually do, how to get started, and who can help. *Marketing Artificial Intelligence* is a smart, sensible, and comprehensive survey of the landscape, full of inspiring examples and practical advice. Whether you are just getting started or already using AI in your marketing, this is a guidebook not to be missed!"
—Jim Lecinski, Clinical Associate Professor of Marketing, Northwestern's Kellogg School of Management and Coauthor of *The AI Marketing Canvas*

"Like Paul, 1 was intrigued with AI, but 1 did not know what 1 did not know. Paul has taken the mystery out of evaluating AI for marketers. Revenue teams are always looking for ways to leverage technology to improve the customer journey for their product or service, and to boost the ROI of their campaigns. With AI's ability to gain insight into your target audience, it is simple to understand why Paul and Mike wrote this valuable book to educate business leaders."

—Jeanne Hopkins, Chief Revenue Officer, OneScreen.
ai and Former VP of Marketing, HubSpot

"A vital roadmap to plan and deploy AI in marketing, regardless of industry or company size. For any CMO or marketing leader who understands the need to innovate quickly with the latest and best technologies, especially in today's digital transformational environment. AI, which is 'more profound than electricity or fire,' will reset marketing completely, and this book is a lifeline for CMOs who think the next five years will look anything like the last five years."

—John Dougherty, Chief Marketing Officer, Brighton Jones

"I consult with hundreds of agency owners every year and I've seen a wide array of reactions to AI from disdain to eager curiosity. Wherever you are on the spectrum—this is the book that will answer your questions, push aside your fears, and illuminate the possibilities. If you want your agency to thrive, continue to be in demand, and be profitable . . . you can't really afford not to read this book. It's written by marketers for marketers. And it is your future."

—Drew McLellan, CEO, Agency Management Institute

Marketing Artificial Intelligence

Also by Paul Roetzer

The Marketing Agency Blueprint
The Marketing Performance Blueprint

Also by Mike Kaput

Bitcoin in Plain English

Marketing Artificial Intelligence

AI, Marketing, and the Future of Business

PAUL ROETZER

with MIKE KAPUT

Matt Holt Books
An Imprint of BenBella Books, Inc.
Dallas, TX

BenBella Books, Inc.
Matt Holt is an imprint of BenBella Books, Inc.
10440 N. Central Expressway
Suite 800
Dallas, TX 75231
benbellabooks.com
Send feedback to feedback@benbellabooks.com

BenBella and *Matt Holt* are federally registered trademarks.

Printed in the United States of America
10 9 8 7 6 5 4 3 2 1

Library of Congress Control Number: 2021062758
ISBN 9781637740798
ISBN 9781637740804

Copyediting by Ruth Strother
Proofreading by Jenny Bridges and Sarah Vostok
Indexing by Debra Bowman
Text design and composition by Aaron Edmiston
Cover design by Brigid Pearson
Printed by Lake Book Manufacturing

Paul Roetzer

*For my mom and dad, whose unconditional support
and love has inspired me to pursue my dreams.*

Mike Kaput

*To Kate, Debbie, and Paul Kaput, without whom
none of this would be possible.*

CONTENTS

Introduction. 1

Chapter 1   The Science of Making Marketing Smart. 9
Chapter 2   Language, Vision, and Prediction. 29
Chapter 3   The Marketer-to-Machine Scale. 39
Chapter 4   Getting Started with Marketing AI 55
Chapter 5   Advertising and AI. 75
Chapter 6   Analytics and AI. 85
Chapter 7   Communications, PR, and AI 95
Chapter 8   Content Marketing and AI 103
Chapter 9   Customer Service and AI 115
Chapter 10   Ecommerce and AI 123
Chapter 11   Email Marketing and AI. 131
Chapter 12   Sales and AI. 139
Chapter 13   SEO and AI. 149
Chapter 14   Social Media Marketing and AI 159
Chapter 15   Scaling AI 169
Chapter 16   More Human 185
Chapter 17   AI and You. 199

Conclusion. 203
Acknowledgments 219
Endnotes. 221
Index. 231

AI is probably the most important thing humanity has ever worked on. I think of it as something more profound than electricity or fire.
—Sundar Pichai, CEO of Alphabet and Google

INTRODUCTION

Marketers write all the rules. They build the plans,
produce the creative, run the promotions, personalize the consumer
experience, and analyze the performance. Traditional marketing is all
human, all the time. But artificial intelligence possesses the power to
change everything.

Your life is already AI assisted, and your marketing will be, too. AI
is forecasted to have trillions of dollars of impact on businesses and the
economy, yet many marketers struggle to understand what it is and how
to apply it to their marketing. As the amount of consumer data expo-
nentially increases, marketers' ability to filter through the noise and turn
information into actionable intelligence becomes more difficult. At the
same time, much of the automation technology marketers rely on today
is elementary and, ironically, largely manual.

Demis Hassabis, cofounder and CEO of DeepMind, defines AI as
"the science of making machines smart," which in turn augments human
knowledge and capabilities. To take inspiration from Hassabis, we have
come to define marketing artificial intelligence as the science of making
marketing smart. With AI, marketers are able to reduce costs by intelligently automating data-driven and repetitive tasks, and to accelerate revenue by improving their ability to make predictions. In addition, AI opens
a new realm of creative possibilities.

Traditional marketing technology is built on algorithms in which
humans code sets of instructions that tell machines what to do. AI has

the potential to define its own rules, determine new paths, and unlock unlimited potential to advance the industry. AI may seem like a futuristic concept, but you use it dozens, if not hundreds, of times every day, and you probably don't even know it. Here are some examples:

- Alexa and Siri answer your questions
- Amazon predicts your next purchase
- Apple unlocks the iPhone by scanning your face
- Facebook targets you with ads
- Gmail finishes your sentences
- Google Maps routes you to your destination
- LinkedIn curates your homepage and recommends connections
- Netflix recommends shows and movies
- Spotify learns the music you love
- Tesla's Autopilot steers, accelerates, and brakes your car
- YouTube suggests videos
- Zoom automatically transcribes your recorded meetings

You don't care that AI powers these experiences, but you do appreciate the convenience and personalization.

While AI has been transforming other industries for decades, and redefining how we learn, communicate, and live as consumers, we have not seen a high volume or velocity of innovations in marketing until now. The same underlying AI technologies—machine learning, deep learning, computer vision, natural language processing, and natural language generation—are accelerating marketing toward an intelligently automated future.

Massive amounts of data, exponential growth in computing power, the availability of AI infrastructure and models from leading technology companies, and the rapidly advancing no-code movement are redefining what is possible for marketers. These factors are combining with a flood of venture capital money to prime the marketing industry for disruption. Many time-intensive, data-driven tasks commonly performed by marketers are being augmented, and in some cases replaced, by AI. Now is the time to evolve your skills, your career, and your business.

The Next-Gen Marketer

This is your chance to be a pioneer in one of the most profound technological shifts in human history. We are in a rare position to create change, to reinvent what it means to be a marketer. You don't have to become a machine-learning engineer or data scientist to take advantage of what AI enables. You simply need to understand what is possible with smarter technologies and apply that knowledge to your business and career.

Learn to look at problems and how to solve them differently so you will be able to drive your organization through the next frontier in digital marketing transformation. Differentiate yourself from your peers by achieving greater efficiencies in your work, building more intelligent campaigns and solutions, and focusing on the traits and abilities that remain uniquely human, such as empathy, creativity, and strategy. You can become a next-gen marketer.

These professionals aren't defined as next-gen because of age, but rather because of their approach to embracing change and applying smarter technologies.

Next-gen marketers know that in order to deliver the personalization and experiences modern consumers expect, marketing must become smarter. It must become *marketer + machine*.

We have entered the age of intelligent automation. AI is not going to replace you. Rather, it will replace specific tasks and augment what you are capable of doing. Don't wait for the marketing world to get smarter around you. Take the initiative now to understand, pilot, and scale AI. The opportunities are endless for marketers with the will and vision to transform the industry.

The marketers who take action have the opportunity to create a significant and sustained competitive advantage for their businesses and themselves. AI enables marketers to:

- Accelerate revenue growth
- Create personalized consumer experiences at scale
- Drive costs down
- Generate greater return on investment (ROI)

- Get more actionable insights from marketing data
- Predict consumer needs and behaviors with greater accuracy
- Reduce time spent on repetitive, data-driven tasks
- Shorten the sales cycle
- Unlock greater value from marketing technologies

AI is all about the outcomes. It is smarter technology that builds smarter businesses.

Discover Your Marketing AI Superpowers

Marketing Artificial Intelligence is an essential guide for next-gen marketers that makes AI approachable and actionable by answering these critical questions:

- What is AI?
- How will AI impact brands?
- Why does AI matter to marketers?
- How is AI altering consumer expectations?
- What can we learn from the intelligent automation of other industries?
- How can marketers use AI to augment their knowledge and capabilities?
- What are the primary AI use cases marketers should be exploring?
- What are the limitations of AI as it exists today?
- Which brands are leading the way in the adoption of AI?
- How can marketers find and assess marketing AI vendors?
- What are the greatest obstacles marketers may face in integrating AI?
- How will marketing jobs evolve?
- Can AI replace marketers now or in the future?
- What skills should marketers learn to stay relevant?
- Are marketing teams ready for AI-powered digital transformation?

- Where should marketers turn for AI education and training?
- What impact will AI have on accelerating revenue growth and reducing costs?
- How should marketers get started with AI?

This book draws on years of research and dozens of interviews with AI executives, engineers, and entrepreneurs. It presents the current potential of AI as of 2022 as well as a glimpse into a future in which marketers and machines work seamlessly together. *Marketing Artificial Intelligence* is designed to help marketers truly understand AI, educate their teams, garner executive support, pilot AI use cases, and develop a near-term strategy for successfully scaling AI. This book largely caters to nontechnical audiences, meaning you don't need a background in analytics, data science, or programming to understand and apply what it teaches.

While AI-powered marketing technologies may never achieve the Hollywood sci-fi vision of self-running, self-improving autonomous systems, a little bit of AI can go a long way to dramatically increase productivity, efficiency, and performance. So rather than fearing AI, marketers must embrace it.

Using AI will give you a competitive advantage. It will give you superpowers. So how do you get started with AI? How do you determine the current and future potential for AI to improve and eventually transform your marketing programs and your career? Come along on a journey of exploration and enlightenment. *Marketing Artificial Intelligence* is the blueprint you've been waiting for to understand and apply AI.

About Marketing AI Institute and the Authors

After more than a decade researching, writing, and speaking about AI, as well as applying it to my businesses, I have come to believe it will be the most transformative technology of our generation. AI will impact every industry and redefine the future of work, business, and society. My small part of that story is to try to advance the marketing industry, to create enough curiosity that marketers of all ages and backgrounds will take the next step to learn what AI is and apply it ethically to their careers and businesses.

In 2016, my coauthor, Mike Kaput, and I teamed up to start a blog and newsletter about marketing AI at www.marketingaiinstitute.com. Mike was working as a senior consultant at my agency, PR 20/20, at the time. We had spent a number of happy hours talking about the future of the industry. When we started exploring how AI would impact our agency and our clients, the conversation quickly moved into more macro-level thoughts around business and society. AI in the marketing industry was not being written about or discussed much in those days, so Mike and I figured maybe we could tell the story of AI in a way that would make it more approachable than much of the technical content that was available. The idea was to share insights from our own learning journeys.

We're not data scientists, engineers, or AI researchers. We're both writers by trade with backgrounds in journalism, marketing, and business. Our thinking was that if we could make AI understandable to ourselves and our team, then maybe we could explain AI to others. That blog grew into a media, event, and online education company with more than forty thousand subscribers as of the publishing of this book. In spring 2021, we raised a $1 million seed round for Marketing AI Institute to advance our mission of making AI approachable and actionable. Along the way, we introduced the Grow Smarter with AI initiative designed to make marketing AI education accessible to all, from college students to CMOs, through AI Academy for Marketers, our e-learning platform (www.marketingacademy.ai).

The Grow Smarter with AI initiative started with making online courses more affordable, but we envision it becoming a movement to help build next-gen marketers and next-gen brands. Our road map is focused on the three primary areas of community, education, and technology. The education element is certainly the furthest along and includes AI Academy for Marketers, Marketing AI Conference (MAICON), the blog, weekly newsletter, monthly webinar series, and the Marketing AI Show podcast as the core programs.

For AI Academy, we're working on delivering AI-powered personalized learning journeys, building more Marketing AI Institute original programming, expanding the network of instructors, and creating deeper specializations for marketing categories and career paths. We're also exploring partnerships with associations and software companies so we can bring AI education to their audiences.

On the technology side, our primary focus has been connecting marketers with AI-powered solutions that can transform their businesses and careers. We've published more than 130 vendor spotlights that profile AI technology companies, offered personalized vendor matches based on use case ratings in our AI Score for Marketers assessment tool (score .marketingaiinstitute.com), hosted on-demand AI Tech Showcase product demos in AI Academy for Marketers, and introduced the AI in Action event series in 2021 to help marketers learn through experience with leading technology companies.

The community aspect is probably the most important element of all, but it's also the earliest in development. The inaugural MAICON in 2019 was our first major effort to bring together a group of like-minded marketers who shared our vision for a more intelligent, more human future. We had three hundred attendees from twelve countries join us in Cleveland, Ohio, that year. But 2020 and 2021 in-person events were lost to the pandemic. We used the pause of offline events to invest energy and resources in bringing marketers together online through our Marketing AI Institute group on Slack as well as connecting them during our MAICON virtual event as best we could. While our community-building efforts have been slow to get off the ground, this community is the future of our organization. Everything we do is about empowering you as a learner and as a leader to transform your career and life through the responsible application of AI. Visit www.marketingaiinstitute.com /community to learn more.

We hope this book stimulates curiosity and becomes a catalyst to drive more marketers to pilot and scale AI. We want to hear from you. Reach out to us on LinkedIn, or email us at book@marketingaiinstitute .com. We'd love to hear your story.

- What are your career aspirations?
- Where are you in your AI journey?

- How can we help you personally evolve and advance?
- What obstacles are you facing in piloting and scaling AI?
- How can we help you drive adoption in your organization?

We don't know where AI is going to take us as an industry, but we look forward to exploring the possibilities together.

Visit www.marketingaibook.com for related resources and downloads.

A Note About First Person Point of View

When reading this book, you will encounter a number of personal stories and anecdotes that Paul wrote from a first person point of view. Any time you read these passages, it is Paul speaking. The first person *we* is also commonly used when representing the thoughts and words of both Mike and Paul as coauthors.

Chapter 1

The Science of Making Marketing Smart

There are more than ten million marketers worldwide according to a simple LinkedIn Sales Navigator job function search. Chances are, since you're reading this book, you're one of them. Of the ten million marketers, four million are entry level, more than one million are marketing managers, and another one million are marketing directors. These professionals are being led by 340,000 marketing vice presidents and 260,000 C-suite executives (CRO, CGO, CMO, etc.). Every marketer has a unique story that helps define the professional (and person) they want to be.

As I scroll through LinkedIn, I find myself wondering why these people chose marketing as their career, what educational backgrounds and job experiences led them to where they are now, and what their aspirations are moving forward. In short, what are their marketing stories?

My story began when I gave premed a shot for about one-quarter of my freshman year in college. I failed. Not for lack of ability, but for lack of trying. As a result, I lost some scholarships, almost lost the privilege to attend Ohio University (my parents were not pleased with my performance), and definitely lost confidence and direction. Then I found my path by doing the only thing I was passionate about at the time—I began to write. Through a mix of long nights (studying this time, instead of partying), second chances, and serendipity, I was accepted into the Ohio University E. W. Scripps School of Journalism spring quarter of my junior year. That same week I was offered my first internship with a public relations and marketing agency in Cleveland, Ohio.

I spent five years at that agency after graduation, then started my marketing firm, PR 20/20, in 2005. The firm became HubSpot's first agency partner in 2007, and then I wrote my first book, *The Marketing Agency Blueprint*, in 2011. That was the same year that IBM Watson, an AI-powered machine, defeated two of the most brilliant contestants the game show *Jeopardy!* had ever seen. I had no idea what artificial intelligence was or how it worked, but I was hooked.

The following year I read *Automate This: How Algorithms Took Over Our Markets, Our Jobs, and Our World* by Christopher Steiner. In the book, Steiner states, "Determining the next field to be invaded by bots is the sum of two simple functions: the potential to disrupt plus the reward for disruption."[1] Steiner went on to write that "some algorithms' roots trace to the field of artificial intelligence. They may not be intelligent and self-aware like Hal 9000 (Heuristically programmed ALgorithmic computer), the machine from the movie *2001: A Space Odyssey*, but algorithms can evolve. They observe, experiment, and learn—all independent of their human creators. Using advanced computer science techniques such as machine learning and neural networking, algorithms can even create new and improved algorithms based on observed results."[2]

I became convinced that AI would transform marketing as we knew it. It would be only a matter of time. Little did I know then that I would spend the next decade obsessed with understanding AI and its applications to marketing, business, and society. That led me to launch Marketing Artificial Intelligence Institute in 2016, create Marketing AI Conference (MAICON) in 2019, introduce the AI Academy for Marketers online learning platform in 2020, and write this book.

The Rate of Change Is Accelerating

These are some of the technologies that did not exist when I graduated from Ohio University in 2000:

- LinkedIn, Facebook, Twitter, Instagram, YouTube, Snapchat, TikTok (i.e., social media)
- iPhone, iPad, iPod, Apple Watch (Apple made computers)
- FaceTime (we didn't even have unlimited voice data plans)
- Gmail (Google itself was only two years old)
- Amazon Alexa (or any voice assistants)
- Bitcoin (or any crypto currency)
- WhatsApp
- Tesla
- Spotify
- Netflix
- Slack

You get the point. Think about how rapidly technology has evolved over the last two decades. Now imagine that multiplied by a factor of ten, twenty, or even one hundred. That is the challenge AI presents. It is accelerating the velocity of change.

> *Software that can think and learn will do more and more of the work that people now do . . . This technological revolution is unstoppable. And a recursive loop of innovation, as these smart machines themselves help us make smarter machines, will accelerate the revolution's pace . . . The coming change will center around the most impressive of our capabilities: the phenomenal ability to think, create, understand, and reason. To the three great technological revolutions—the agricultural, the industrial, and the computational—we will add a fourth: the AI revolution.[3]*
> —Sam Altman, CEO of OpenAI

So are marketers ready for this next frontier in digital marketing transformation? Unfortunately, our research shows they are not. In the

"2021 State of Marketing AI Report," we learned that marketers see a near-term intelligently automated future and believe AI will be essential to their success, but understanding and adoption of AI are slow to take hold.[4]

There is a common belief that fear of AI and the unknowns it presents to the workforce is an obstacle that must be overcome to achieve widespread adoption. Yet we found the majority (56 percent) of marketers believe AI will create more jobs than it eliminates over the next decade. And when asked specifically about barriers to the adoption of marketing AI, only 16 percent chose fear of AI as a contributing factor.

So if not fear, then what is it that is preventing marketers from evolving? It is a lack of education and training, as reported by 70 percent of respondents. To further this point, when asked if their organization has any AI-focused education and training, only 14 percent of the respondents said yes. AI is forecasted to have trillions of dollars of impact on businesses and the economy, yet the majority of marketers struggle to understand what it is and how to apply it to their marketing.

So let's start from the beginning.

What Is Artificial Intelligence?

Ask ten different experts to define AI, and you will likely get ten different definitions. My favorite, in part because of its simplicity, is the definition by Demis Hassabis we referenced in the introduction: "the science of making machines smart." These machines, in turn, enhance human knowledge and capabilities. Yes, they sometimes replace humans as well, but we'll get to that later.

So, with Hassabis's definition in mind, we can think of marketing artificial intelligence as "the science of making marketing smart."

Now if you're new to AI, even these basic definitions are a bit abstract. They don't help you understand the difference between AI and all the other related terms you hear, such as *machine learning, natural language processing, natural language generation, deep learning, neural networks,* and *computer vision.* So let's break this down a little further.

Basically, AI is the umbrella term for the algorithms, technologies, and techniques that make machines smart and give marketers superhuman capabilities. Machines, which we use throughout the book to mean the hardware and software you use every day to do your job, are relatively simple and unintelligent. These machines are programmed, by humans, to execute tasks. They don't get better on their own, and they don't make you better at your job, unless you take the initiative to continually advance your own abilities.

Now consider your marketing technology stack. You likely have dozens of software solutions you rely on to drive performance. These solutions are constantly being updated with new features that you and your team need to learn in order to maximize the technology's value and the ROI of your marketing programs. It is almost impossible for marketers to stay current as the rate of technology accelerates. Therefore, we are all performing below our potential.

But what if marketing success didn't rely solely on marketers advancing their own knowledge and capabilities? What if the machine itself learned and constantly improved? Enter machine learning, the primary subset of AI.

Machine learning is literally a system that learns. It takes in structured (e.g., names, dates, addresses, numbers) or unstructured (e.g., text, images, videos, voice) data, discovers insights, and finds patterns that marketers would often miss (or never think to consider), and then makes predictions, recommendations, and, in some cases, decisions.

Although you may not realize it, you make predictions all day long as a marketer. From what subject line to use in an email, to what time to schedule the social share, to what image to use in the advertisement, to what price to include in the promotion. With every decision, you are subconsciously trying to predict what will get another human to take a desired action. You just often use instinct and educated guesses instead of science and math.

The most important element of machine learning, and what truly differentiates it from traditional statistics and computer science, is that it continues to evolve and improve based on new data. In other words, it gets smarter. The human still tells the machine what to predict and, in most cases, decides what to do with those predictions. But machine learning can give marketers superpowers when it has the right data. This has implications in every area of marketing where data lives, including analytics, automation, advertising, content, email, sales, search, social, and websites.

It's easiest to understand AI by looking at specific challenges and use cases. Let's take the case of an e-book used for lead generation. When someone downloads an e-book, a marketer defines a set of rules that tells the machine what to do next. For example: *If visitor downloads e-book, then send three-part email.* This set of if-then rules is called an algorithm. In isolation, setting a single rule for a single download is straightforward.

However, what if there are ten thousand downloads across five personas originating from multiple channels (social, organic, paid, direct) that require personalized emails and website experiences based on user history and intent signals? Humans are unable to conceive of the optimal set of instructions to guide a machine to personalize thousands of unique experiences. This is where AI excels. It takes data-driven, repetitive tasks, and makes them look easy. But AI doesn't stop at setting up the initial rules to maximize performance. It uses machine learning to constantly evolve. In other words, it learns, it gets smarter, and it creates its own algorithms. Now imagine the potential if all the repetitive tasks you complete, and the data-driven decisions you make every day as a marketer, were intelligently automated, and then consider if that was only the beginning.

Deep Learning Comes of Age

Deep learning is a subset of machine learning. A simplified explanation is that deep learning takes different approaches to emulating how the human brain learns and works in order to give machines the ability to see, hear, speak, write, move, and understand.

The reality is that scientists don't really know that much about how the human brain works and how it is so efficient. But researchers have made significant progress applying what they do know to advance what machines are capable of achieving. What scientists have discovered is that things that are easy for humans are often difficult for machines.

For example, when you teach a toddler what a dog is, that child learns and can recognize dogs with ease for the rest of his or her life. For a machine to learn what a dog is, you have to train it using millions of images of dogs. After enough training, it can identify dogs with reasonable accuracy, but it still doesn't actually know what a dog is. The machine uses what are called neural nets to analyze an image through different layers (such as a layer for size, a layer for color, a layer for shape, a layer for fur) and predict that what it is "seeing" is what it was trained to identify as a dog. It may even be able to generate a description of the dog using its knowledge base of language-training data. But the machine has never played with a dog. It doesn't understand the human connection to dogs. It doesn't know whether to fear them or to love them. The machine can't truly understand what a dog is because it has no emotions, no feelings, no consciousness, no soul. The machine represents and understands the world through bits of data. To a machine, something is either a 0 or 1. Something either is, or it is not.

The machine is not actually intelligent. It is artificially representing intelligence by performing mathematical calculations at superhuman levels. But when a machine has lots of data and immense computing power, it can achieve remarkable feats. It can do humanlike things at superhuman levels. Deep learning is what makes that possible.

Much of the deep-learning story has unfolded since 2011 as the technology began to move from decades of academic theory and false hopes to practical commercial applications across industries. Major technology companies are now in a race for AI talent and supremacy, largely fueled by the potential for deep learning to transform the future of business. You see deep learning at work in search results, voice assistants, text generation, translation, facial and image recognition, and hundreds of other consumer-facing technologies. But deep learning also lies hidden in the infrastructure of companies, powering more intelligent operations and unlocking previously unimaginable levels of cost efficiency and revenue acceleration.

In January 2021, Mark Cuban, billionaire entrepreneur and investor, shared his thoughts about the critical nature of AI to businesses today in a series of tweets.

AI dominance may not be obvious in a product or service. It's everything that is done to optimize the things you don't see, from pricing, mfg, customer service, etc. These lead to better cash flows. It's a new paradigm in organizing companies but it's INCREDIBLY HARD to do right.[5]

The "AI Squad". The companies that have harnessed AI the best are the companies dominating. To paraphrase a great movie line, "They keep getting smarter while everyone else stays the same." It's the foundation of how I invest in stocks these days. "How good is the company at AI."[6]

To understand the significance of deep learning to the future of marketing and business, it helps to consider how some of the world's most innovative companies are infusing AI into every aspect of their businesses, and building cloud services with pretrained AI models that can drive your digital transformation.

In the remainder of this chapter, we explore the AI history and ambitions of Amazon, Google, and Microsoft, and show you how the education, resources, and cloud services provided by these tech giants can rapidly accelerate your AI understanding and adoption.

AI Terms to Know

The field of AI comprises many disciplines, technologies, and subfields. There are dozens of terms that are used to describe AI technologies, and the definitions can be complex and confusing. These are some common terms and simplified definitions to help you advance your understanding of AI.

- Artificial Intelligence: The science of making machines smart.
- Marketing AI: The science of making marketing smart.
- Algorithm: Set of rules that tell a machine what to do.
- Traditional Automation: Automation powered by sets of instructions (aka algorithms) coded by humans that tell machines what to do.
- Intelligent Automation: Automation powered by AI that has the potential to define its own algorithms, determine new paths, and unlock unlimited potential.
- Machine Learning: The primary subset of AI in which the machine uses data to continually learn and make more increasingly accurate predictions.
- Deep Learning: An advanced type of machine learning that mimics the functioning of the human brain, giving machines humanlike abilities to see, hear, write, speak, understand, and move.

Amazon

What started out as personalized recommendations for books and other products through its ecommerce site has expanded into a dizzying array of AI applications across all aspects of Amazon's business. From robots in its warehouses, to voice-powered assistants in millions of consumer devices, to its dominant cloud-computing business that powers AI for other organizations, there are few companies in the world that have embraced AI like Amazon.

While onstage at the Code Conference in June 2016, famed technology journalist Walt Mossberg asked Amazon founder Jeff Bezos about the role of AI in technology moving forward. Bezos replied, "I think it's gigantic." In regards to natural language understanding, machine learning, and AI, Bezos said, "It's probably hard to overstate how big of an impact it's going to have on society over the next 20 years."[7] He went on to say that "the combination of new and better algorithms, vastly superior compute power, and the ability to harness huge amounts of training data" were the three things coming together that would enable businesses to solve previously unsolvable problems while creating "a tremendous amount of utility" for customers that would drive adoption.

When Mossberg asked Bezos if he was deeply committed to AI being a huge part of their business, Bezos replied that what they were doing was "just the tip of the iceberg of what you can do with these kinds of technologies." In Bezos's mind, the world had only reached the first inning of what was possible with AI and "might even be the first guys up at bat." Bezos felt society was on the "edge of a golden era."

It is hard to believe that six years have passed since that Code Conference interview, but Bezos's premonitions about the impact of AI have certainly come true for Amazon. Amazon Web Services (AWS), the company's cloud-computing platform, accounted for more than $16.1 billion in revenue during third quarter 2021.[8] For comparison, Google Cloud reported $4.99 billion during the same quarter.[9]

AWS delivers machine-learning services and supporting cloud infrastructure to more than one hundred thousand customers. According to the AWS website, "AI Services provide ready-made intelligence for your applications and workflows to help you improve business outcomes—based on the same technology used to power Amazon's own businesses. You can build AI-powered applications without any machine learning expertise."[10]

While most marketers will likely need at least some support from developers and data scientists to implement Amazon's AI solutions, any marketer can explore the pretrained models and understand the potential they hold. Here are some examples:

- Amazon Comprehend is a natural language processing (NLP) solution that uses machine learning to find and extract insights and relationships from documents.
- Amazon Forecast combines your historical data with other variables, such as weather, to forecast outcomes.

- Amazon Kendra is an intelligent search service powered by machine learning.
- Amazon Lex is a solution for building conversational interfaces that can understand user intent and enable humanlike interactions.
- Amazon Lookout for Metrics detects and diagnoses anomalies in business and marketing data, such as unexpected drops in sales or unusual spikes in customer churn rates.
- Amazon Personalize powers personalized recommendations using the same machine-learning technology as Amazon.com.
- Amazon Polly converts text into natural-sounding speech, enabling you to create applications that talk.
- Amazon Rekognition makes it possible to identify objects, people, text, scenes, and activities in images and videos.
- Amazon Textract automatically reads and processes scanned documents to extract text, handwriting, tables, and data.
- Amazon Transcribe converts speech to text.
- Amazon Translate uses deep-learning models to deliver accurate, natural-sounding translation.

AWS also offers solutions by industry, including advertising and marketing. Within the industry offerings are segments for marketers, agencies, and advertising technology. According to the website, "AWS has over a decade of experience helping companies handle virtually any cloud workload for advertising & marketing—especially in key areas such as marketing data lakes, advertising analytics, audience platforms, customer data platforms, personalization, messaging, and digital customer experience."[11]

When you want to see what's next at Amazon, you can check out Amazon Science (www.amazon.science), the company's research arm focused on AI innovation and invention in the areas of computer vision, conversational AI and NLP, machine learning, information and knowledge management, search and information retrieval, and robotics.

Google

Sergey Brin and Larry Page first met in the summer of 1995 when Page visited Stanford University, and Brin, then a second-year computer science graduate student, served as his guide. Soon thereafter, Page chose Stanford and a doctoral thesis topic that would change marketing, business, and the world as we know it.[12]

Page was fascinated at the time by the World Wide Web, which was just starting to explode with information and possibilities. As a computer scientist, he saw the web as a classic graph structure in which computers were the nodes and web page links were the connections between the nodes. Within this graph model, he saw the potential for backlinks to add credibility to web pages, much like citations do in academic papers. So Page set out to count and qualify each backlink on the web as part of a project he called BackRub. At the time, the web consisted of approximately ten million documents, compared to the more than one billion active websites today.

Brin became intrigued by what Page was working on and teamed up with Page on the project. Together, they created a transformative algorithm known as PageRank (named after Larry Page) that considered both the number and quality of inbound links to each website. They hadn't set out to create a better search engine than that of Yahoo!, Lycos, Excite, or AltaVista, the dominant search companies of the day, but that is exactly what they achieved. Brin and Page would go on to found Google in 1998 and publish "The Anatomy of a Large-Scale Hypertextual Web Search Engine," in which the conclusion states:

> *Google is designed to be a scalable search engine. The primary goal is to provide high quality search results over a rapidly growing World Wide Web. Google employs a number of techniques to improve search quality including page rank, anchor text, and proximity information. Furthermore, Google is a complete architecture for gathering web pages, indexing them, and performing search queries over them.*[13]

By late 2002, two years before an IPO that would value the company at $23 billion, Google had expanded to five hundred employees and was generating about $100 million in annual sales powered by its search engine and advertising business. At around that time, Page would hint at Google's AI-first future in an interview with *PBS NewsHour*:

> *The ultimate search engine . . . would understand exactly what you wanted when you typed in a query, and it would give you the exact right thing back, in computer science we call that artificial intelligence. That means it would be smart, and we're a long way from having smart computers.*[14]

Fast forward to 2017: Google was now the largest subsidiary of a new parent company named Alphabet, and AI had been infused into seemingly every aspect of Alphabet's operations and products. In the annual Alphabet Founders' Letter, penned by Brin that year, he talked about how "the power and potential of computation to tackle important problems" had never been greater. Brin went on to write:

> *[The] most important factor is the profound revolution in machine learning that has been building over the past decade . . . The new spring in artificial intelligence is the most significant development in computing in my lifetime. When we started the company, neural networks were a forgotten footnote in computer science; a remnant of the AI winter of the 1980s. Yet today, this broad brush of technology has found an astounding number of applications. We now use it to:*

- *Understand images in Google Photos*
- *Enable Waymo cars to recognize and distinguish objects safely*
- *Significantly improve sound and camera quality in our hardware*
- *Understand and produce speech for Google Home*
- *Translate over 100 languages in Google Translate*
- *Caption over a billion videos in 10 languages on YouTube*
- *Improve the efficiency of our data centers*
- *Suggest short replies to emails*
- *Help doctors diagnose diseases, such as diabetic retinopathy*

- *Discover new planetary systems*
- *Create better neural networks (AutoML)*
- *. . . and much more*[15]

Brin added that he expected machine-learning technology to continue to evolve rapidly and that he intended for Alphabet to continue to be a leader in the space.

The following year, Sundar Pichai, who had become Google's CEO, expanded on the company's AI ambitions and long-term vision, saying, "We are fortunate to have a timeless mission, and the way we approach it continues to evolve. Each phase change has been the result of careful, long-term planning that began by placing big bets in areas we believed would pay big dividends for society 5, 10, even 20 years down the road. One good example is our early bet on AI."[16]

He continued to describe how Google created its own powerful tensor processing units specifically to advance the speed and efficiency of its machine-learning capabilities. This technological advancement in computing power contributed to a remarkable milestone achieved by DeepMind, a deep-learning company Google acquired in 2014 for $650 million. DeepMind defeated the world's human Go grandmasters with its AlphaGo computer program. The historic AlphaGo match in 2016, in which the machine defeated world champion Lee Sedol four to one, was watched by more than two hundred million people and ushered in a new era in deep learning.

The success of AlphaGo led Pichai to write, "At that point it became clear to me that we were in a unique position to advance the field because we had an amazing team of AI researchers and the computational power required to sustain the work." He went on to say that "those early investments put us in a strong position to shift the company to an AI-first strategy, and we have pursued that rigorously across our products to better serve our users. One of our clearest insights on AI so far is that its potential is greatest when paired with human intelligence . . . We believe that we can develop AI in a way that complements human expertise, and we feel a deep responsibility to get this right."[17]

While Brin and Page have both since retired from the internet giant, Pichai, the CEO of both Alphabet and Google since 2015, has left no doubt about the impact he believes AI will have on business and society. When he appeared onstage at the 2018 World Economic Forum, Pichai boldly stated something he has repeated time and again: "AI is probably the most important thing humanity has ever worked on. I think of it as something more profound than electricity or fire."[18]

As a marketer, you are impacted by Google's AI everyday while engaging and influencing consumers through Gmail, Google Search, Google Ads, Google Maps, Google Assistant, and YouTube. Plus, you likely experience Google's machine learning and NLP at work with Google Analytics, Google Docs, and Google Sheets. And with Google Cloud, as well as a bit of help from your engineering and data-science teams, you can build on Google's AI solutions to add the following sight, language, conversation, and structured data into your applications:

Sight
- Vision: Derive insights from images
- Video: Enable content discovery such as object recognition and create engaging experiences through highlight reels, recommendations, and interactive elements

Language
- Translation: Dynamically detect and translate between languages
- Natural Language: Reveal the structure and meaning of text through machine learning

Conversation
- Dialogflow: Build virtual agents and other conversational experiences
- Text to Speech: Convert text to humanlike speech using WaveNet voices
- Speech to Text: Convert speech to text automatically with a high degree of accuracy

Structured Data

- AutoML Tables: Automatically build and deploy state-of-the-art machine-learning models on structured data; some advanced support may be needed with this solution
- Recommendations AI: Deliver highly personalized product recommendations
- Cloud Inference Application Programming Interface (API): Quickly run large-scale correlations over typed time-series datasets[19]

If you want to keep tabs on what's to come from Google, you can join the 1.5 million people who follow the Google AI research team on Twitter (@GoogleAI). According to Jeff Dean, Google senior fellow who heads up Google AI, the company wants "to use AI to augment the abilities of people, to enable us to accomplish more and to allow us to spend more time on our creative endeavors."[20]

The Google AI team regularly publishes its research in academic journals, releases projects as open source, and applies advances to Google products. The core areas of research include:

- Algorithms and theory
- Data management
- Data mining and modeling
- Human-computer interaction and visualization
- Machine intelligence
- Machine perception
- Machine translation
- Natural language processing
- Robotics
- Security, privacy, and abuse prevention
- Speech processing

Given Google's aggressive investment in AI, the company's products and solutions will continue to evolve at a rapid pace and push the boundaries of what is possible with AI.

Microsoft

In 2004, Microsoft cofounder Bill Gates went on a university campaign tour of sorts in an effort to stimulate interest in computer science in general, and the profession of software engineering in particular. Following the dot-com bubble burst, and amid a growing trend of software programming jobs being sent abroad, the number of students majoring in computer science was falling. That year, the Computing Research Association's annual survey of more than two hundred universities in the United States and Canada found that undergraduate enrollments in computer science and computer engineering programs were down 23 percent.[21]

Whereas many thought the computing industry had reached its maturity, and opportunities to build meaningful businesses and careers in computing were fading, Gates believed the best was yet to come. "Computer science is about to be able to accomplish things that people have been working on for decades," he said, referring to how the field was on the verge of technological breakthroughs in AI.[22]

When one student asked if it would ever be possible to build another technology company as successful as Microsoft, which at the time had a $268 billion market cap, Gates replied, "If you invent a breakthrough in artificial intelligence, so machines can learn, that is worth 10 Microsofts."

As of December 2021, Microsoft's market cap sits at $2.4 trillion, roughly nine times its 2004 size, and artificial intelligence specialist is the fastest growing profession in the United States, according to the "LinkedIn 2020 Emerging Jobs Report."[23]

Microsoft CEO Satya Nadella called AI the "defining technology of our times"[24] and stated that Microsoft's objective is to be able to turn every industry into an AI-first industry by enabling companies to convert their data in secure, privacy-preserving ways into AI capabilities that generate real business returns and drive digital transformations.[25]

During the 2018 Microsoft Inspire event, Nadella said, "We are going to infuse everything with AI. It's going to have perception capability, language capability and autonomy that's going to be built into the applications going forward."[26] He went on to explain how advances in deep learning had enabled Microsoft and others to achieve human-level parity in the domains of machine reading and comprehension as well as machine translations. He outlined Microsoft's ambition to enable every brand to build true conversational interfaces while democratizing and accelerating autonomy everywhere.

Microsoft's Azure cloud-computing service is the key to bringing this vision to life. Azure AI enables companies to build solutions that can analyze images, comprehend speech, make predictions using data, and imitate other intelligent human behaviors. Within Azure AI is Cognitive Services, which is a collection of domain-specific pretrained AI models that can be customized with a company's data. Microsoft breaks its Cognitive Services into four primary categories: decision, language, speech, and vision.[27]

Decision: Make smarter decisions faster
- Anomaly Detector: Identify potential problems early on
- Content Moderator: Detect potentially offensive or unwanted content
- Personalizer: Create rich, personalized experiences for every user

Language: Extract meaning from unstructured text
- Language Understanding: Build natural language understanding into apps, bots, and Internet of Things devices
- QnA Maker: Create a conversational question and answer layer over your data
- Text Analytics: Detect sentiment, key phrases, and named entities
- Translator: Detect and translate more than ninety supported languages

Speech: Integrate speech processing into apps and services
- Speech to Text: Transcribe audible speech into readable, searchable text
- Text to Speech: Convert text to lifelike speech for more natural interfaces

- Speech Translation: Integrate real-time speech translation into your apps
- Speaker Recognition: Identify and verify the people speaking based on audio

Vision: Identify and analyze content within images and videos
- Computer Vision: Analyze content in images and video
- Custom Vision: Customize image recognition to fit your business needs
- Face: Detect and identify people and emotions in images

Beyond Azure, Microsoft has an AI Lab that lets you explore and experience AI and also offers an AI Business School with free on-demand education designed to help organizations address the opportunities and challenges when embracing AI.

Beyond the Big Three

While the AI stories of Amazon, Google, and Microsoft give us a sense of the significance of what is happening, these companies are not alone in their ambitions. Every major technology company is competing for talent and collectively pouring billions of dollars into AI research and the acquisitions of upstart AI companies. Alibaba, Apple, Baidu, IBM, Meta, NVIDIA, Salesforce, and Tencent are just some of the other organizations to follow as innovations emerge seemingly every day from every corner of the world.

Chapter 2

Language, Vision, and Prediction

One of the biggest challenges I faced as a marketer trying to comprehend artificial intelligence was finding practical applications and use cases that made the technology seem less abstract and more actionable. I felt that if I could understand what the broad categories of AI were, then it would be much easier to identify use cases for myself and to teach other people how to pilot and scale AI in their businesses. So a few years back, I decided that a good way to do that was to study how Amazon, Google, and Microsoft were defining and categorizing AI.

As we saw in chapter one, the three companies have different products and services, and they brand their AI solutions and research in different ways. But I noticed a pattern emerging that seemed generally to fit most AI applications relevant to marketing today. The three broad categories I identified were language, vision, and prediction. Within those categories are dozens of AI applications that can be used to make marketing smarter. And within those dozens of AI applications are thousands of use cases that can drive efficiency and performance in your business. We will explore use cases in chapters five to fourteen. This chapter is focused on the top-level categories and common applications.

The good news for marketers is that AI terminology is generally literal, as you will see in the definitions that follow. We have chosen to keep our definitions in this book as simple and understandable as possible, and we have tried to avoid more technical jargon that can distract from our goal of helping you achieve a baseline understanding of AI. Once you start to comprehend these applications, you can begin to think about all the ways you can use AI in your marketing. You will also start to recognize the AI that is present within the business and marketing technologies you use every day.

Let's take a closer look at each of these categories and applications.

Language

Language is the ability of machines to understand and generate written and spoken words. Here are some sample AI applications within the language category:

- Natural Language Processing (NLP): Processing human language so the machine understands what is being written or said
- Natural Language Generation (NLG): Generating written or spoken language
- Sentiment Analysis: Understanding the meaning of words, specifically whether the words are positive, negative, or neutral
- Speaker Identification: Recognizing who is speaking
- Speech to Text: Turning spoken word into written word
- Text Analysis: Analyzing written words
- Text Extraction: Identifying and extracting objects, such as names, places, dates, and numbers
- Text Generation: Generating written words
- Text to Speech: Turning text into spoken words
- Translation: Translating one language into another
- Voice Generation: Generating spoken words
- Voice Recognition: Recognizing voices

Voice assistants are a great example to consider in the language category. Siri, Alexa, Google Assistant, and Cortana would not be possible without AI. When you talk to Alexa, the machine uses NLP to understand and process what you are saying to it. Amazon also uses voice profiles so you can train Alexa to know who is speaking (i.e., speaker recognition). And when the machine talks back to you, it's using NLG.

Now keep in mind, as we learned in chapter one, a machine does not have any of these humanlike capabilities without AI. But once it's trained, it can, in theory, perform some humanlike functions at superhuman speeds and with human-level (or better) accuracy. And through the power of machine learning, the machine continually evolves and improves. To understand the potential power of AI in this category, think of all the ways language plays a role in any marketing function that has to do with writing, speaking, or listening. Now imagine that a machine could intelligently automate or augment all your daily tasks and marketing programs in which language is analyzed or generated.

Project Copyscale

In April 2015, I launched an internal initiative at PR 20/20 named Project Copyscale. It was designed to answer one seemingly straightforward question: Can we automate content creation with AI? More specifically, can we use machines to write blog posts?

Like most organizations, we were struggling to create content at scale while maintaining quality. I had just returned from the South by Southwest Conference in Austin, Texas, where I heard the managing editor of the *Associated Press* and the CEO of Automated Insights discuss how the *Associated Press* had used Automated Insights technology to shift earnings reports to 100 percent machine written. I had also spent the better part of three years theorizing and building prototype software that would use AI to automate marketing strategy. So I knew theoretically what was possible, but I had no idea if the technology existed to transform our agency, the marketing industry, and the business world at large.

What we learned after acquiring an Automated Insights license was that the answer, at that time, was a resounding no. While Automated Insights did automate the creation of data-driven content, and saved our team dozens of hours every month writing analytics reports, it was not AI. It was human-powered automation.

With Automated Insights, our team of copywriters learned to program templates that told stories based on structured datasets (i.e., rows and columns in a spreadsheet). Each row of data was a potential narrative. Once you learned how to envision and structure the story, you could generate content at scale. This formulaic writing capability is perfect for data-driven content such as earnings reports, analytics briefs, product descriptions, real estate property listings, and press releases. This was how the *Associated Press* went from producing three hundred earnings reports per quarter written by humans, to more than three thousand per quarter written by machines. Impressive, but not intelligent.

But that was 2015, before major breakthroughs in deep learning altered the trajectory of language applications.

What Happens to Marketing When AI Can Write Like Humans?

There is a race to train AI systems to generate human language at scale. When achieved, the implications, both good and bad, are immense. OpenAI, an AI research company originally backed by billionaire technology leaders like Elon Musk, Peter Thiel, and Reid Hoffman, builds AI models to do just that. It started with generative pretrained transformers called GPT and GPT-2. These are AI language generation models that automatically produce human-sounding language at scale.

GPT-2 wowed the world when it was released in 2019 with its ability to construct long-form content in different styles using huge amounts of content from the internet. The GPT-2 model had such substantial implications for malicious use that OpenAI originally chose not to release the trained model. The organization's hope was that by limiting the release, the AI community would have more time to discuss the larger effects of such systems.

Yet in May 2020, OpenAI introduced a dramatically more powerful model called GPT-3 that was able to produce humanlike text. In early experiments, the model was used to produce things such as coherent blog posts, press releases, and technical manuals, often with a high degree of accuracy. To do that, GPT-3 uses 175 billion parameters in its language model, compared to GPT-2's 1.5 billion.

GPT-3 is still in its early days as of 2022, and the validity of the model has not been fully explored. But the speed of improvement in OpenAI's language models should be top of mind for every marketer, writer, and business leader. The first GPT model came out in 2018. GPT-2 was released with greatly expanded capabilities in 2019. Just a year later, GPT-3 uses one hundred times as much data as its predecessor and is beginning to display incredible content creation capabilities, including turning text into code and evaluating investment memos.

This technology provides major opportunities and challenges for marketers. Microsoft has a $1 billion exclusive licensing deal with OpenAI for GPT-3, and at the time of this writing, there are more than three hundred language generation startups powered by GPT-3.[28]

In the near future, brands may be able to build AI-powered content programs at scale. They may also be able to dramatically reduce the costs associated with content creation. But brands will have to be wary of bias that comes with AI content models. It is all too easy for AI models to accidentally generate discriminatory or offensive content. Content at scale sounds great on paper but becomes difficult to police in practice.

What happens to content creators when AI can automatically generate humanlike content at scale? We are optimistic AI will create more jobs in the marketing industry at large than it will make obsolete. But should this technology become widely available, professionals who predominantly create content may need to reevaluate their roles and skills.

The full story of GPT-3 and similar language generation models is just beginning and much is still unclear. But the story provides the starkest example yet of just how powerful certain types of AI have become, and how they could seriously impact brands and marketers.

Vision

Vision is the ability of machines to analyze and understand data from still images and videos. In essence, computer vision seeks to automate tasks that the human visual system can naturally do. Here are sample AI applications of vision:

- Emotion Detection: Detecting human emotion in photos and videos
- Image Recognition: Identifying images in photos
- Facial Recognition: Recognizing faces in photos and videos
- Movement Detection: Detecting movement in spaces
- Video Recognition: Recognizing images in videos

As with language, the vision application names have literal meanings, so it's not hard to comprehend what they are. The magic comes in knowing what to do with the technology to improve your marketing and business. For example, Talkwalker, a conversational intelligence platform, uses image recognition and video recognition to monitor logo and product appearances in photos and videos.[29] Previously, a human would have to manually tag videos and images with brand and product names for media placement to be discoverable. Now AI intelligently automates the process without time-intensive, human-generated tagging.

You experience the convenience of vision applications every day when you use facial recognition to unlock your iPhone, share GIFs that have been automatically tagged with image recognition, and discover recommended videos on social media thanks to video recognition. While the marketing uses of vision may not be as obvious as that of language applications, the only real limitation is your imagination.

How Can AI Inspire Our Creativity?

We like to think that creativity remains a uniquely human capability. While that may be true for now, there is no denying that AI holds the power to enhance and inspire our creativity. Consider the Salvador Dalí deepfake (a combination of *deep learning* and *fake*) experience at the Dalí Museum in St. Petersburg, Florida.

According to the *Verge*, "the exhibition, called Dalí Lives, was made in collaboration with the ad agency Goodby, Silverstein & Partners (GS&P), which made a life-size re-creation of Dalí using the machine learning–powered video editing technique. Using archival footage from interviews, GS&P pulled over 6,000 frames and used 1,000 hours of machine learning to train the AI algorithm on Dalí's face. His facial expressions were then imposed over an actor with Dalí's body proportions, and quotes from his interviews and letters were synced with a voice actor who could mimic his unique accent, a mix of French, Spanish, and English."[30]

The exhibit is designed to humanize Dalí through personalized experiences with visitors. The virtual Dalí engages audiences through stories about his life and even takes selfies with them that visitors can then receive via text.

Amazingly, the technology is readily available to create experiences like this. Nathan Shipley, GS&P technical director, said that he pulled the deepfake code off GitHub, an online community used by developers to collaborate and share code.

The Dalí installation is a great example of what is possible with AI. But in order to tap into its potential, you have to understand the technology and what it is capable of doing.

The Danger of Deepfakes to Your Brand

Vision can also be applied to produce deepfake videos in which a person in an existing image or video is replaced with someone else's likeness. The prevalence and impact of deepfake videos is just beginning, and having an understanding of the underlying technology will help you prepare your brand for its potential impact.

I did a fair amount of crisis communications planning early in my career. Basically, you envision different scenarios of what could go wrong, then put strategies in place for how the organization will react. Then, you hope none of it actually happens. Never did I imagine a day in which brands would be planning for deepfake videos of executives doing and saying things that never happened in real life. But, here we are.

AI has made it possible—and relatively easy with the right resources—to create fake videos of people that appear and sound real. According to Siwei Lyu, who works for the Defense Department developing software to detect and prevent the spread of deepfakes, "it only takes about 500 images or 10 seconds of video to create a realistic deepfake."[31] That means all those social media photos and YouTube videos your company shares could be used against your brand. So the next time you meet with the PR team to talk about crisis communications, make sure to put deepfake videos on the agenda.

Prediction

Prediction is the ability of machines to predict future outcomes based on historical data. With machine learning, predictions continually evolve and improve based on new data. The better the data that goes in (the inputs), the better the predictions that come out (the outputs). Prediction is probably the most relevant category to you right now, as it has the potential to improve your decision-making across every area of marketing and business. Here are sample applications of prediction:

- Forecasting: Predicting business outcomes
- Pattern Recognition: Identifying patterns in data
- Personalization: Personalizing experiences
- Recommendation: Making recommendations to achieve desired outcomes

One of my favorite books about AI is *Prediction Machines: The Simple Economics of Artificial Intelligence*. The authors state that "at low levels, a prediction machine can relieve humans of predictive tasks and so save on costs. As the machine cranks up, prediction can change and improve decision-making quality. But at some point, a prediction machine may become so accurate and reliable that it changes how an organization does things. Some AIs will affect the economics of a business so dramatically that they will no longer be used to simply enhance productivity in executing against the strategy; they will change the strategy itself."[32]

The Untapped Power of Prediction in Marketing

As we have discussed, the simplest way to understand AI is to think about it as a set of technologies and algorithms that are designed to make machines smart, to give them humanlike capabilities (e.g., vision, hearing, speech, writing, understanding, movement). Specifically, machine learning, the primary subset of AI, makes machines smarter at making predictions. And sometimes what may seem like a simple prediction on the surface can have an immeasurably profound impact on the future.

For example, the effort to build truly autonomous vehicles, which would transform society and save millions of lives, is insanely complex. However, when you break autonomy down to its most basic goal, companies like Tesla are trying to build AI systems that predict what a good, focused human driver would do. So the autonomous system does not have to be programmed for every situation; it just needs to learn through billions of miles of training what a good human driver would do.

Predicting human behavior and outcomes is at the heart of everything we do as marketers. Consider the case of an email promotion. Every task related to the planning, production, and distribution of the email comes down to making decisions based on what we predict will influence behavior that will achieve our goal. This includes subject line, images, lede, length, colors, personalization tokens, send time, calls to action, and more.

What if you could customize every one of those elements down to an individual recipient level based on real-time data? Rather than relying on industry best practices and instinct, you could deliver an email campaign with the highest probability of creating value for the recipient and achieving your goals. AI-powered prediction enables personalization at scale, and it makes you a smarter strategist and decision maker.

Augmenting Your Business with AI

As you are thinking about the value of AI, consider all the ways that the language, vision, and prediction applications featured in this chapter can augment your products, strategies, and decision-making to help you build a smarter business.

Now let's put this knowledge to work and learn how to assess AI vendors in chapter three.

Chapter 3

The Marketer-to-Machine Scale

The auto industry has a clever way of categorizing levels of automation in a vehicle. At its core is a simple question: What does the human in the driver's seat have to do?

Society of Automobile Engineers International's J3016 Levels of Driving Automation,[33] as it is known, has become the industry standard for rating how autonomous a vehicle is.

For Levels 0–2, the human is driving. Even if there are support features activated, such as a blind spot warning, the human is making the decisions and is in control. However, when a car reaches Level 3, the machine is able to drive itself under select controlled conditions. At Level 5, technically the steering wheel is no longer needed. The machine can drive itself in all conditions without human input or oversight. Level 5 does not exist as of 2022, but that is the goal of some car manufacturers in the near future. Now J3016 does not talk about artificial intelligence in its scale, but autonomy would not be possible without it.

To give you some context, Tesla cars with Autopilot are considered Level 2 today.[34] A Tesla can drive itself in some conditions, such as on the freeway, but the driver must constantly supervise the support features.

While it is not fully autonomous, Tesla is powered by sophisticated AI, specifically computer vision that lets it "see" the road and the surrounding environment, and assist the driver with getting from point A to point B. But the point here is this is only Level 2. There is also a very important distinction to what is happening in the Tesla that carries over into what we are going to talk about in the marketing industry, and that's the human in the loop.

Human in the Loop

I bought a Tesla Model S in September 2018. When I got the car, the semi-autonomous technology at the time was in essence glorified cruise control. The Model S would stay behind the cars in front of me at a preset distance that I defined. It would slow down and accelerate, and it would stop itself to avoid accidents or if it sensed the driver was not paying attention. But little by little the car would get smarter through over-the-air updates that Tesla regularly pushes out to its fleet, the same way smartphone manufacturers push out updates to their devices.

Over time, the Model S learned to alert me to construction cones, display different car types around me based on sizes and shapes, recognize motorcycles and pedestrians, and even recommend lane changes. The lane change improvement was one of the most fascinating to me because it clearly showed the use of machine learning at work.

When Tesla's lane change assistance was first enabled, the system would use the eight onboard cameras to read the speeds of all the cars around the Tesla and then a prompt would appear recommending a lane change if it predicted a faster path. The driver would get to say yes or no to the recommendation. I found it to be a potentially helpful feature, but it didn't really add that much convenience to the driving experience. And, honestly, it was a bit unnerving to let the car change lanes by itself. However, what most drivers didn't realize was that their actions and decisions were being used to provide inputs that would train the system to know when to change lanes on its own and to more closely emulate the behaviors of the human driver.

About a month or two after Tesla's launch of the lane change assistance feature, a new update arrived that enabled the driver to allow their car to change lanes without their input. Tesla had learned from its training data that its AI was as good as or better than a human driver at knowing when to change lanes. Using Autopilot, a driver could now enter a destination, get on the highway, and the car would then drive itself, with human oversight, to the highway exit, at which point the human driver would take back full control.

So how did this happen? Tesla uses machine learning to monitor and learn from every mile driven by more than one million Tesla vehicles in the company's fleet. Each car is constantly taking in data about what the human driver is doing and whether they are accepting the recommended lane changes. Once Tesla is confident that its vehicles can recommend lane changing as well as or better than a human, Tesla can push that update to their cars. That is how Tesla continually improves the autonomous system within its cars. It learns in the background, constantly recording what is happening, and it uses machine learning to improve the software's predictions and recommendations, therefore improving what the car is capable of doing.

The Technical Side of Tesla AI

If you are interested in the more technical explanation of how Tesla AI works, here's how the company explains it:

We develop and deploy autonomy at scale. We believe that an approach based on advanced AI for vision and planning, supported by efficient use of inference hardware, is the only way to achieve a general solution to full self-driving . . .

Neural Networks
Apply cutting-edge research to train deep neural networks on problems ranging from perception to control. Our per-camera networks analyze raw images to perform semantic segmentation, object

> detection and monocular depth estimation. Our birds-eye-view networks take video from all cameras to output the road layout, static infrastructure and 3D objects directly in the top-down view. Our networks learn from the most complicated and diverse scenarios in the world, iteratively sourced from our fleet of nearly 1M vehicles in real time. A full build of Autopilot neural networks involves 48 networks that take 70,000 GPU hours to train. Together, they output 1,000 distinct tensors (predictions) at each timestep.[35]

The reason I explain all this about Tesla is to demonstrate a real-world case study of how AI works and to help you think about AI in the context of marketing software. What software are you using to do your job every day that gets smarter at regular intervals? I'm not talking about new features you have to learn in order to get value from them. I'm talking about intelligently automated capabilities that make you better at your job without having to invest the time to take a course or read the help section to understand and apply. How much more enjoyable could your job be if every piece of software you used was constantly learning and making recommendations that saved you time and money and increased the probability of you achieving your goals? That is the promise of AI in marketing.

We are years away from AI being seamlessly infused into every marketing technology, but you can buy smarter solutions today for specific use cases that will help your organization reduce costs and accelerate revenue. You just need to know how to find and assess AI technology. To do that, you can take inspiration from the simple question asked in the automotive industry when determining levels of automation: What does the human in the driver's seat have to do?

What Will the Machine Do? What Will the Marketer Do?

Since we launched Marketing AI Institute in 2016, I've wanted a simple, universally accepted way to evaluate marketing AI technology. Not based on the sophistication of the AI but rather on the level of intelligent automation (i.e., AI plus automation) that the AI enables and the value that intelligent automation creates for an organization.

Why is the level of intelligent automation more important than the level of sophistication when evaluating AI technology? Consider Google Gmail's Smart Compose. Smart Compose finishes sentences for you by predicting what word or words you will type next. This technology was years in the making for Google. It requires deep-learning algorithms, tons of data, and lots of computing power, but in terms of the intelligent automation of the task of writing an email, it's pretty minimal. It can certainly improve your writing, and maybe make you a bit more efficient, but it still requires you to provide information, including who you are sending the email to, the subject line, when you want to send it, if you want to add attachments, and often the start of each sentence to prompt the AI to predict what's next. Plus you have to accept or reject each recommended word or phrase.

So when you are buying AI-powered technology, it's critical to remember that AI does not replace you; it augments your knowledge and capabilities to different degrees. In essence, you are trying to determine what the machine will do and what the marketer will do.

To help visualize this idea, we created the Marketer-to-Machine (M2M) Scale that classifies five levels of intelligent automation at the use case level. In other words, we're not trying to rate an entire company or platform but a specific AI technology for a narrowly defined application or task.

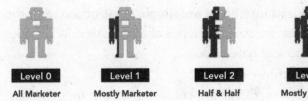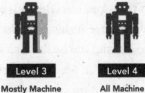

| Level 0 | Level 1 | Level 2 | Level 3 | Level 4 |
| All Marketer | Mostly Marketer | Half & Half | Mostly Machine | All Machine |

The M2M Scale is designed to help marketers assess the true cost and potential of AI-powered tools. By understanding which M2M level a technology enables, you are better able to determine how it will impact your business and your team, and the full scope of work required to adopt and scale the technology. It's important to remember that a little bit of AI can go a long way in reducing costs and driving revenue when you have the right data and use cases. You don't need to go from fully manual to fully autonomous to see massive returns.

Let's take a look at the M2M Scale levels of intelligent automation. For each level, we show common tasks associated with the use case of publishing an email newsletter. All ten tasks have the potential to be intelligently automated to some degree with AI technology that exists today. As the level increases, more of the work is being done by a machine.

Level 0: All Marketer

All human, all the time. The system does not use any AI and is only capable of doing what it has been instructed to do. All automation is manual.

Level 1: Mostly Marketer

Limited intelligent automation. The system uses AI in certain aspects, but it is largely reliant on marketer inputs and oversight. At Level 1, the machine may be able to do the following: curate popular resources from across the web and create a subject line.

Level 2: Half & Half

About half marketer, half machine. The system can manage most aspects of the use case but still requires marketer inputs and oversight. This includes all Level 1 tasks plus the following: write the copy, personalize each email based on user preferences and interests, and send the email.

Level 3: Mostly Machine

Predominantly AI powered. The system can operate without human inputs or oversight in select conditions. This includes all Level 2 tasks plus the following: plan the content, choose the audience lists, monitor performance, and generate a performance report with key performance indicators (KPIs) and insights.

Level 4: All Machine

Full autonomy. The system can perform at or above human level without inputs or oversight. The marketer simply defines the desired outcome, and the machine does all the work. This includes all Level 3 tasks plus the following: improve content, design, and personalization based on performance data.

Much of the marketing technology you use today is Level 0: all human, all the time. You plan and execute everything, and the software does what you tell it to do. The software does not learn, it does not improve, and it does not make you better at your job.

Most AI-powered marketing solutions on the market today enable basic to moderate levels of intelligent automation and fit into Levels 1 or 2. Level 3 is possible but likely only after a significant investment of time and inputs during planning, training, and onboarding phases. Level 4 does not exist in marketing today.

So how do you determine how intelligently automated AI technology really is? You will need to consider four variables.

Information, Oversight, Dependence, and Improvement

As we have discussed, AI needs information, or inputs, to learn and perform its tasks. Inputs commonly are in the form of structured or unstructured data that the human provides to the machine. For example, rather than A/B testing various digital ads, we use an AI technology to predict the success of our digital ad creatives before we launch a campaign and spend a single dollar. Pattern89's AI learns from the performance of millions of previous ads (the inputs) to predict which version of our creatives will have the highest probability of driving engagement.

The next variable is oversight, or the level of training, monitoring, and intervention the machine needs. If you think back to the Tesla example, the system still requires significant oversight from the driver. The driver is monitoring the road at all times, and they actually have to put their hands on the wheel, usually every fifteen to thirty seconds, so that the machine knows that they are paying attention. The same concept holds true with AI-powered marketing technologies today. You don't just turn it on and forget it. You actually have to spend time and energy overseeing the AI and training it to do what it does.

That leads to the next variable: dependence, or how reliant the machine is on the marketer to complete its objective. The ultimate vision for AI is to give it a goal, say, generate five hundred leads this quarter, and it determines how to achieve it. But that's not how the current generation of AI technology works in marketing, nor are we anywhere near that level of autonomy. The machine needs the human to be in the loop to have the greatest probability of producing results.

The final variable is improvement, or the process by which the machine learns and improves. So again with the Tesla example, we know that it's monitoring the human's driving, and it's learning through the onboard cameras that are constantly taking in new data. It then processes that data to improve the software, and then those improvements get pushed to all users.

Now imagine if your marketing automation platform was constantly getting smarter. It could recommend changes to email nurturing campaigns based on user behavior, alert you to outdated or ineffective workflows, suggest target accounts, adapt lead scores in real time based on conversion data, learn individual contact preferences, surface personalized content to website users, and continuously analyze performance data to discover insights and anomalies. This could allow you to focus on the uniquely human stuff, like strategy and creativity.

Here are the key variables that determine the M2M levels:

- Inputs: The information needed to perform the task
- Oversight: The amount of training, monitoring, and intervention that is needed
- Dependence: The level of the machine's reliance on the marketer to complete its objective
- Improvement: Ways the machine learns and improves

How to Vet AI Vendors

AI is just smarter marketing technology, but it's what you should be demanding from the vendors in your tech stack. We have profiled more than 130 AI-powered vendors on our blog (bit.ly/marketing-ai-blog), and we continually track the activities and funding of more than one thousand. In the process, we've learned what it is about the state of marketing AI tech that makes it challenging for marketers to assess and buy the right solutions.

First, there is a significant lack of product maturity in the market. Many of the AI-powered vendors have emerged since 2016 and have raised a bunch of money on the promise of AI. They may have .ai in their domain names, but their AI capabilities are often still early and unproven.

Just because marketing technology companies claim they use AI, machine learning, or deep learning, doesn't necessarily mean their solutions are actually much more intelligent or efficient than what you are already using. Oftentimes, some form of AI—such as NLP—is used in limited features within a product, but the solution as a whole probably isn't as advanced as the marketing messages may lead you to believe.

This leads to the second challenge: overhyped branding. The vendors want to tout their AI features to differentiate their technology from traditional solutions, as they should. The problem occurs when the vendors exaggerate what their AI is capable of doing. A general rule of thumb we follow is to assume that any vendor who claims to be the first or the only is neither, and if their site states that something is fully autonomous, it's not.

Many marketing technology companies are just starting to experiment with AI, and while they may have road maps for more integration of AI moving forward, it's still early. So they are in a tough spot. They want to tout the intelligent elements of their products, but they don't want to overpromise what they will deliver in the short term.

Which takes us to the third challenge: a lack of AI education in vendor marketing and sales teams. This is what often results in the overhyped branding. Basically, since the marketers don't fully understand the underlying technology, they struggle to explain it in simple terms for customers and prospects. They tend to focus on what it is and what it does (often just using talking points from the engineers), rather than what the technology makes possible and why it's smarter than traditional marketing technology.

This all causes a big disconnect in the market and creates confusion and frustration on both ends. The best way to approach evaluating AI technology is to always start with a business case. This can be as simple as providing a short explanation of why this technology and vendor are being evaluated. Ideally include the business problem that is being solved, or a summary of the value expected to be gained by intelligently automating related use cases. Here's an example:

> Our team spends more than fifty hours per month manually developing content strategy and optimizing posts to grow our audience. Continued expansion of audience and leads are critical to achieving our department and business goals, and we have identified intelligent automation of content strategy as a primary use case to drive success.
>
> This vendor is one of the leaders in the content intelligence space. With more than $50 million in funding and a G2 Crowd rating of 4.5, it has a number of AI-powered features we believe can drive efficiency in our processes and campaigns.

Once you have the business case, you can move into vetting specific vendors through demos and audits. In the next section, we offer a collection of questions you should research before buying AI technology to get a clear understanding of how it can impact your business. If you can't find the answers through your own discovery work, don't hesitate to ask the vendors directly. If they don't have good answers to your questions, then they may not be the right fit for your company.

These questions are organized into three categories: vendor, technology, and team.

Questions About the Vendor

What is the vendor's point of view on AI?

When it comes to vendors, one of the most important considerations is their public point of view on AI. If you're investing in marketing technology, you want to see a clear explanation from their top leadership about their investment in AI and how they see it impacting your business. Think back to the examples of Amazon, Google, and Microsoft in chapter one. The CEOs are regularly speaking and writing about AI, they have AI-specific products and services, and they run research labs dedicated to the advancement of AI.

Does the vendor have a public road map for its AI capabilities?

Ask vendors about their plans for continually making their software smarter, and, in turn, making you better at your job. This is especially important when evaluating solutions that are core to your technology stack, such as marketing automation, customer relationship management (CRM), project management, and content management system (CMS).

Buy marketing software that is core to your company's success only from vendors who are committed to deep integration of AI technology. It's not an option but an imperative for marketing software companies to be AI-first. Otherwise, they will become obsolete, and you will be at a competitive disadvantage.

What training and onboarding are provided?

Some of the most innovative marketing AI applications come from venture-funded startups whose customer success programs are still early in development. As a result, your team may not have access to the formal training needed to get the full value from the technology. So it's important to understand what resources the vendor provides to onboard and guide your people.

What is the vendor's position on ethics in AI?

If you're going to be trusting technology to help you make decisions and engage and influence your audiences, you better be confident in the ethical standards and practices of the vendor from which you are buying. The vendor should be able to clearly state and demonstrate its policies on the ethical development and use of AI. See chapter sixteen for important context and resources related to the ethical use of AI in your business.

How does the vendor help customers maintain security and compliance?

AI is powered by data. Be confident in the security and compliance practices of your technology partners to protect your company's and customers' data.

Who are the vendor's ideal customers in terms of company size and industries?

As with any marketing technology purchase, you want to be confident that the AI solutions are a fit for your organization.

Questions About the Technology

How does the vendor use AI (i.e., machine learning, NLG, NLP, deep learning, etc.) in its products?

When assessing the overall value of a marketing technology, it helps to understand which features are AI powered and which are still all human powered. For example, when we were selecting a virtual event platform for MAICON 2021, we demoed five leading platforms. Only one of them, Swapcard, offered any AI-powered features to enhance the networking experience by intelligently matching attendees. The rest of the platform features were comparable to the competition, but Swapcard was taking an AI-first approach to networking, and did an excellent job explaining how AI works on their site, so it was the obvious choice.

What are the primary marketing use cases for the company's AI-powered solutions?

You want to know specifically which tasks you will be able to do smarter with their technology. For example, if you're considering a language generation solution powered by GPT-3, such as Jasper (www.jasper.ai) or CopyAI (www.copy.ai), you will evaluate how many of your regular writing tasks will be augmented by the machine writing. At the time of this writing, Jasper has more than fifty templates for crafting website copy, videos, ads, emails, blogs, and social media posts, and CopyAI has more than eighty language-generating tools.

What makes the vendor's AI-powered solutions smarter than traditional approaches and products (i.e., how does the vendor drive efficiency and performance)?

All the AI in the world is irrelevant if it doesn't help you do your job faster, better, or cheaper (preferably all of the above). Just ask the vendor point-blank how the technology is smarter than your traditional approach. Explain your current process, how much time it takes, the quality of the output, and the impact it has on your business. Then have the rep walk you through how the AI technology will improve each of those steps.

Using the M2M Scale, what level of intelligent automation can we expect in the beginning? What level can we reach over time?

Be clear on how intelligently automated the technology will really make your use case. Consider the amount of inputs and oversight that will be required of your team, and know how the solution will get smarter over time. Again, most AI technologies will be in the Level 1 (Mostly Marketer) or Level 2 (Half & Half) range, with the potential to get to Level 3 (Mostly Machine) over time. If they say it is Level 4 (All Machine), then they are misleading you or misinformed about their products' true abilities. In that case, we recommend you find a different vendor.

Are there any minimum requirements (e.g., for data or list size) to get value out of the technology?

Ask what amount of data is needed for the AI solution to be viable. Lead scoring is a great example here. Machines excel at making predictions about conversions and continually evolving scoring based on new data. But there is usually a minimum threshold needed, say two thousand conversions per month, before the machine learning can really take hold and achieve the level of accuracy that will make your team confident that it is better than human-built models.

What data does it use?

Going back to the topic of ethics in AI, it's important that you know where their training data comes from (assuming it's not your first-party data), how it is acquired, and whether there are any inherent biases in the data. Most marketers are not going to be confident in their ability to assess this area, so you may want to pull in a data scientist to help you make sense of the information and give you peace of mind. See chapter sixteen for more on ethics and bias in AI.

What do you see as the limitations of the technology as it exists today?

As we covered earlier in this chapter, AI can definitely be overhyped by vendors. Just be direct when asking about current limitations. For example, in the language-generation space, there are lots of promises being made about what AI can do, but our experience to date has been that most applications require far more training and oversight than the vendors let on in their messaging.

What are common obstacles to adopting the technology?

Once you purchase the technology, what are the challenges you will face to achieve adoption within your organization? Back to the lead-scoring example, if in the early stages of adoption your sales team perceives the leads being recommended by the machine are not good, they may just revert back to their own systems before the AI has the chance to learn and improve. Knowing this, you will want to provide education and training to your sales team so they understand how the technology works and give it the time needed to learn.

How does it learn and improve over time?

If the technology is not getting smarter and making you better, then it is not worth the investment. Ask the vendor how the machine learns and how often improvements are pushed to you as the end user.

Does it integrate with _____?

This question is critical. AI solutions are built to perform specific tasks. So in theory, you could be adding dozens of new products to your marketing tech stack. If these AI solutions do not integrate with your core platforms, either out of the box or through third-party systems such as Zapier, then you could quickly create complexity and friction in your operations. Plan ahead and look for AI solutions that are already part of your core stack's ecosystem.

Questions About Your Team

What kind of in-house capabilities do I need?

There is a big movement toward no-code or low-code solutions that give the average marketer the ability to leverage AI without needing any coding experience. However, that doesn't necessarily mean you will have all the capabilities on your team to implement the new AI solutions. Data scientists are often essential, as are more technical operations professionals and developers who can lead the integration and adoption of different solutions.

What training is needed for our team? Does the vendor provide it?

AI solutions can seem abstract, overwhelming, and, in some cases, intimidating to marketers who do not understand the technology or how they will work with it. Ideally, vendors provide educational resources and training specific to the AI capabilities of their products.

Will we need additional outside support to use the technology?

If you don't have all the necessary capabilities in-house, or the vendor doesn't provide adequate training for your team, then you may need to turn to consultants and agencies for help. In this case, find out if the vendor can recommend partners who are trained and certified in using the product.

What does a standard onboarding process look like?

The amount of training needed for your team and the machine will impact what a standard onboarding process looks like. Unfortunately, AI rarely delivers on its value proposition out of the box. Be sure to understand the time to value (TTV) so you can set realistic expectations and goals with your team.

What regular tasks will your team be required to complete?

As the AI learns and improves and moves along the M2M Scale, forecast which tasks will remain human powered and which machine-powered activities will continue to require human oversight. This will give the information to scope the true cost and value of AI over time.

All AI Is Not Created Equal

The more you understand AI and what to look for, the greater chance you have of finding the right technologies that create value for your company.

Challenge AI vendors to explain in simple terms how their technology works and how it is smarter than what you are doing now. Ask them how it will save time and money and increase your likelihood of achieving success. If the sales rep can't talk in plain terms about the value of their AI, then ask to have one of the engineers walk you through it. The general rule of thumb is don't buy it if you don't understand it. After all, AI is not magic; it's math.

So the next time you're doing a product demo with an AI-powered vendor, ask them to clearly define for you what the machine will do and what the marketer will do. Have them provide onboarding and ongoing management checklists so that you can create a true scope of work for what it will take to adopt and scale the technology. And consider both how the M2M level may change over time as you invest more resources in the technology, and how the vendor uses data to make the solution smarter.

Now that you understand how to sort the signal from the noise in AI technology, it's time to get started with it yourself. It's time to find your own personalized use cases for AI in your marketing organization.

Chapter 4

Getting Started with Marketing AI

By summer 2016, my fleeting fascination with artificial intelligence had given way to a full-blown obsession. Inspired by hundreds of AI articles and reports, a series of online courses, and a collection of related books, the narrative of how AI would impact marketing started to take shape in my mind. I saw it as essential to both our agency and the industry, but I wasn't sure what to do next.

When faced with telling complex stories, I have always found it best to start with an outline. In the case of AI, I began working on an outline for a new book. I wanted to take readers on a journey from the origins of AI to a future in which humans and machines worked seamlessly to run personalized marketing campaigns of unprecedented complexity with unimaginable simplicity.

The challenge of creating the book outline was in the middle part of the story. I realized I had no idea what marketers could actually do with AI at the time. I didn't know which of the AI-powered tech startups were legitimate, and it was becoming increasingly difficult to cut through all the noise and hype. Suddenly everyone was inserting *AI*, *machine learning*, and *deep learning* into their messaging, but it wasn't clear how much more intelligent and efficient their solutions really were.

In addition, it became increasingly apparent that intelligently automating marketing would require dozens of individual tools. That's because AI is narrow in its capabilities and must be purpose-built to do one thing at a time. In other words, there is no marketing AI platform that neatly bundles everything into a single monthly subscription.

While all the major players in marketing automation and CRM were starting to build and buy AI capabilities, we were still years away from an artificially intelligent marketing platform. So by fall 2016, I was left with an incomplete book outline. I thought I knew the beginning and the end, but I was missing the most important part: today. What do we do now? How do marketers get started with AI?

The 5Ps of Marketing AI

In November 2016, we launched Marketing AI Institute to try and figure out the story of AI in marketing and share what we were learning with anyone who was also curious. I wanted to hear directly from the entrepreneurs and engineers building AI tools about what the use cases and limitations were, how they were using AI in their products, and what types of organizations were applying and benefiting from AI already. So as part of our editorial calendar mix, we started regularly publishing vendor spotlights on the blog, where we asked the same nine questions of every AI-powered marketing technology company:

1. In a single sentence or statement, describe your company.
2. How does your company use AI in its products?
3. What are the primary marketing use cases for your AI-powered solutions?
4. What makes your AI-powered solution smarter than traditional approaches and products?
5. Are there any minimum requirements (e.g., data, list size) for marketers to get value out of your AI-powered technology?

6. Who are your ideal customers in terms of company size and industry?
7. What do you see as the limitations of AI as it exists today?
8. What do you see as the future potential of AI in marketing?
9. Any other thoughts on AI in marketing or advice for marketers who are just getting started with AI?

These questions were chosen to make AI more approachable and actionable for readers, but also to help us figure out where the industry really was in terms of AI adoption. The insights gained from this research also led to the creation of a new framework to help visualize and organize the marketing AI technology landscape—the 5Ps of Marketing AI.

First presented during my Content Marketing World 2017 session, "Machine-Assisted Narrative," the 5Ps are still considered to be a beta framework. It will evolve as the market shifts and as we develop a deeper understanding of AI and its implications on the industry. The 5Ps are as follows:

1. Planning: Building intelligent strategies
2. Production: Creating intelligent content
3. Personalization: Powering intelligent consumer experiences
4. Promotion: Managing intelligent cross-channel promotions
5. Performance: Turning data into intelligence

The 5Ps framework was originally designed to broadly cover the entire marketing process, and it became the foundation for an interactive tool to help marketers identify use cases and technologies within each area.

AI Score for Marketers

Once we had the 5Ps framework to work with, the next step in our minds was to figure out the common use cases. We believed that if we could define tangible ways to apply AI, then it would be much easier for marketers to see the potential and begin adopting smarter technologies. This led to the creation of AI Score for Marketers (bit.ly/ai-score-marketers), a free online assessment tool that enables you to explore and rate dozens of AI use cases and get personalized recommendations for AI-powered vendors.

Originally released in 2018, version two features thirteen survey questions and forty-nine sample AI use cases for you to rate using the 5Ps framework. In each section—Planning, Production, Personalization, Promotion, Performance—you are asked the same question: Assuming AI technology could be applied, how valuable would it be for your team to intelligently automate each use case? Use cases are rated on a 1 to 5 scale (1: no value, 2: minimal value, 3: moderate value, 4: high value, 5: transformative). For each use case, you consider the potential time and money saved and the increased probability of achieving business goals.

Upon completing the assessment, you immediately unlock access to your AI Score results page, which surfaces all use cases you rated 3 to 5, and provides personalized vendor match recommendations based on your ratings. If we have published a vendor spotlight on the company, then clicking the Learn More link takes you right to that article. You also receive an overall AI Score as well as section-by-section scores that are designed to help prioritize your research in the areas you value highest.

The assessment takes seven to ten minutes. Contact information is not required to get your results, but if you try it out, be sure to include your email address on the Profile page if you want to periodically receive benchmark reports, assessment version updates (in case you want to check out new use cases and vendors), and alerts for educational opportunities and events.

"2021 State of Marketing AI Report": Top Use Cases

Marketing AI Institute and Drift, a leader in conversational commerce for B2B companies, teamed up in fall 2020 to gain unparalleled insights into the awareness, understanding, and adoption of AI throughout the marketing industry. Using AI Score for Marketers and the 5Ps framework, respondents had the opportunity to rate the value of the forty-nine sample marketing AI use cases. More than 400 marketers answered portions of the survey, and 235 completed all questions and use case ratings.

Across all use cases, the average rating was 3.53 out of 5.00. As a part of the survey, respondents were given an overall AI Score based on the total value of their ratings divided by 245, which is the total possible score if you rated every use case a five. This score is a reliable proxy for understanding AI's potential for an organization across each of the 5Ps, as well as an individual's overall need for AI in their marketing. The assumption is the higher you score, the more you value the potential of intelligent automation in your marketing.

Across all respondents, the average total AI Score was 71 percent, indicating AI holds overall high potential for the marketing activities of those surveyed. We also broke down the AI Score for each individual use case category.

Following are the average ratings from the 2021 report. Every one of these use cases is possible today with AI technology that already exists. So if you see a use case that would rank high for you, just jump into your favorite search engine and enter (or say), "AI for [use case]." There is a good chance you will find multiple vendors that have built AI solutions for that exact case.

Planning: Building intelligent strategies

The average AI Score across planning use cases was 68 percent, slightly below the overall average. The average use case rating in this category was 3.41. Planning use cases, with average ratings, include the following:

- (3.78) Choose keywords and topic clusters for content optimization
- (3.75) Analyze existing online content for gaps and opportunities
- (3.69) Score leads based on conversion probabilities
- (3.54) Construct buyer personas based on needs, goals, intent, and behavior
- (3.53) Identify companies and contacts to target in sales and account-based marketing campaigns

- (3.49) Map buyer journey stages based on historical lead and conversion data
- (3.47) Define topics and titles for content marketing editorial calendars
- (3.44) Prescribe strategies and tactics to achieve goals
- (3.43) Determine campaign goals based on historical data and forecasted performance
- (3.31) Gain insights into competitors' digital ad spends, creatives, and strategies
- (3.30) Guild media and influencer databases based on interests, audiences, and intent
- (3.19) Predict customer churn
- (3.15) Formulate pricing strategies to maximize profitability
- (3.14) Allocate and adjust marketing budgets
- (2.91) Find and merge duplicate contacts in your CRM

Production: Creating intelligent content

The average AI Score across production use cases was 71 percent, the same as the overall average. The average use case rating in this category was 3.52. Production use cases, with average ratings, include the following:

- (3.82) Create data-driven content
- (3.77) Optimize website content for search engines
- (3.70) Predict content performance before deployment
- (3.69) Send email newsletters with personalized content
- (3.57) Curate content from multiple sources
- (3.52) Design websites, landing pages, and calls to action
- (3.49) Draft social media updates with copy, hashtags, links, and images
- (3.48) Analyze and edit content for grammar, sentiment, tone, and style
- (3.45) Write email subject lines
- (3.45) Develop digital advertising copy
- (3.42) Tag website images with keywords and categories
- (3.32) Write creative briefs and blog post drafts

- (3.14) Transcribe audio (calls, meetings, podcasts, webinars) into text

Personalization: Powering intelligent consumer experiences

The average AI Score across personalization use cases was 73 percent, above the overall average. The average use case rating in this category was 3.64. Personalization use cases, with average ratings, include the following:

- (3.96) Recommend highly targeted content to users in real time
- (3.74) Determine offers that will motivate individuals to action
- (3.74) Present individualized experiences on the web and/or in app
- (3.59) Customize email nurturing workflows and content
- (3.45) Optimize email send time at an individual recipient level
- (3.37) Engage users in conversations through bots that learn and evolve

Promotion: Managing intelligent cross-channel promotions

The average AI Score across promotion use cases was 73 percent. The average use case rating in this category was 3.65, which was the highest across categories. Promotion use cases, with average ratings, include the following:

- (3.92) Adapt audience targeting based on behavior and look-alike analysis
- (3.81) Predict winning creatives (e.g., digital ads, landing pages, calls to action) before launch without A/B testing
- (3.80) Deliver individualized content experiences across channels
- (3.62) Adjust digital ad spend in real time based on performance
- (3.52) Improve email deliverability
- (3.47) Identify real-time social media and news trends for promotional opportunities
- (3.44) Schedule social shares for optimal impressions and engagement

Performance: Turning data into intelligence

The average AI Score across performance use cases was 72 percent, higher than average. The average use case rating in this category was 3.61. Performance use cases, with average ratings, include the following:

- (3.91) Measure ROI by channel, campaign, and overall
- (3.86) Discover insights into top-performing content and campaigns
- (3.80) Forecast campaign results based on predictive analysis
- (3.63) Create performance report narratives based on marketing data
- (3.51) Predict revenue potential for accounts at different stages of the buyer journey
- (3.50) Receive real-time alerts based on unusual changes or trends in your marketing data
- (3.43) Determine which teams, channels, and campaigns get credit for conversions
- (3.21) Monitor and evaluate brand mentions from media and influencers

The top ten individual use cases by score across all 5Ps were as follows:

1. Recommend highly targeted content to users in real time (3.96)
2. Adapt audience targeting based on behavior and look-alike analysis (3.92)
3. Measure ROI by channel, campaign, and overall (3.91)
4. Discover insights into top-performing content and campaigns (3.86)
5. Create data-driven content (3.82)
6. Predict winning creatives (e.g., digital ads, landing pages, calls to action) before launch without A/B testing (3.81)
7. Forecast campaign results based on predictive analysis (3.80)
8. Deliver individualized content experiences across channels (3.80)

9. Choose keywords and topic clusters for content optimization (3.78)
10. Optimize website content for search engines (3.77)

Another way to think about use cases is as marketing categories or disciplines. Out of the top ten use cases above, three would fit in the content marketing category. An additional three would be classified as analytics use cases. The third most common category of use case was SEO, comprising two out of the top ten use cases.

Chapters five to fourteen present dozens of use cases and vendors organized by marketing categories. So if you're looking for ideas to get started in specific areas such as advertising, communications and PR, email marketing, and social media, you will find lots of inspiration in those sections of the book.

Finding Your Top Use Cases

It's important to remember that use cases are subjective. Since AI Score lets each individual rank the use cases based on their own perceived value to intelligently automate a task, a low-ranked use case for one marketer may have the potential to unlock enormous value for others.

For example, the second lowest rated use case in the 2021 report—transcribe audio (calls, meetings, podcasts, webinars) into text—was instrumental in the writing of this book. We started book production by cataloging every content asset, and then used Descript and Otter.ai to transcribe every relevant online course, webinar, podcast, presentation, video, and interview we have done since 2016 that had not already been converted into text. This resulted in more than one hundred thousand words that served as the foundation of the manuscript.

We do the same thing for each podcast and webinar as they are published, using the resulting transcripts to quickly create blog posts and social shares. The next step for us is to find AI-powered content summarization technology that can read and understand the transcriptions and extract the key messages to summarize each piece of content we publish.

Our plan was to use content summarization technology to write summaries for each book chapter. However, at the time of this writing, we were not able to find a vendor offering this as an out-of-the-box solution. We expect that to change soon as the applications for that sort of technology are massive in marketing and business.

The AI Score use cases are meant to be a starting point. There are hundreds, if not thousands, of marketing AI use cases to consider that could be valuable to your organization. So how do you figure out which use cases are right for you?

Piloting AI

When you are getting started with AI and looking to build internal support, you will want to focus your investments on quick-win pilot projects with a narrowly defined scope and high probability of success. Specifically, you are looking for use cases that are data-driven, repetitive, and predictive.

Thousands of activities marketers perform every day, such as audience targeting, content strategy, SEO, media buying, email writing, and predicting conversions and churn, will be intelligently automated to some degree in the near future. The key is to think about everything your team does regularly, and then consider two primary factors:

1. The value to intelligently automate (value rating) all or portions of that activity, with value being defined by potential time and money saved and the increased probability of achieving business goals
2. The ability to intelligently automate (ability rating) the activity based on existing AI technology or solutions that could be built with the right resources

Keep in mind that a little bit of AI can go a long way to reduce costs and drive revenue when you have the right data and the right use case. The key is finding use cases that matter to you and your team. We've created the *Piloting AI Workbook* that you can access to help identify and prioritize your use cases. Visit www.marketingaibook.com to download the Excel file.

The workbook contains ten columns in the template:

1. 5Ps: Choose the 5Ps category from the dropdown
2. Marketing Category: Select the relevant marketing category
3. Task: Enter the use case
4. Interval: Indicate how frequently you complete the task
5. Estimated Hours Per Month: Estimate how much time you spend on the task
6. Existing Technology: Add what technology, if any, you currently use to complete the task
7. Estimated Monthly Cost: Fill in costs related to the technology
8. Build or Buy: Indicate if you would likely build or buy the AI solution (if known at this point)
9. Value to Intelligently Automate: Select on a scale of 1 to 5, with 1 having no value and 5 being transformative, how valuable it would be to intelligently automate the task
10. Ability to Intelligently Automate: Select on a scale of 1 to 5, with 1 being low and 5 being high, the ability to intelligently automate the task

The workbook contains a tab with sample use cases you can reference as a starting point, and you can look back at the "State of Marketing AI Report" use cases as well.

The Problem-Based Model

Whereas starting with use cases is the fastest way to pilot AI and create efficiencies in your marketing, the problem-based model will likely have a greater long-term impact on enterprise value. In this model, you have a known pain point or challenge that may be solved more efficiently and at scale with AI. Your team follows a fact-based, hypothesis-driven methodology to solve the problem. Following are the ten steps in the problem-based model. They are broken into two phases: discovery, in which the problem is defined and validated, and planning, in which strategy is established to resolve the problem.

Phase 1: Discovery

1. Define the problem statement

What is the challenge that will be solved? The problem statement is defined at this step and becomes the foundation of the project. Here is a sample problem statement:

> The company has more than one hundred thousand email addresses and has sent more than one million emails in the last twelve months, but open rates remain low at 8 percent, and sales attributed to email have remained flat since 2018. Based on current averages, a 2 percentage-point lift in email open rates could produce a $50,000 increase in sales over the next twelve months.

It's important to note that a strong and valid problem statement should include the value of solving the problem. This helps ensure that the project is worth the investment of resources and keeps everyone focused on the goal.

2. Build and prioritize the issues list

What are the primary issues causing the problem? The issues are categorized into three to five primary groups and built into an issues tree. Sample issues could be:

- Low open rates
- Low click rates
- Low sales conversion rates

3. Identify and prioritize the key drivers.

What factors are driving the issues and problem? Sample key drivers could include:

- List fatigue
- Email creatives
- Highly manual, human-driven processes
- Underutilized or missing marketing technology solutions
- Lack of list segmentation
- Lack of reporting and performance management
- Lack of personalization

4. Develop an initial hypothesis

What is the preliminary road map to solving the problem? Here is a sample initial hypothesis:

AI-powered technologies can be integrated to intelligently automate priority use cases that will drive email efficiency and performance.

5. Conduct discovery research

What information can we gain about the problem, and potential solutions, from primary and secondary research?

- How are talent, technology, and strategy gaps impacting performance?
- What can be learned from interviews with stakeholders and secondary research related to the problem? Ask questions such as the following:
  - What is the current understanding of AI within the organization?
  - Does the executive team understand and support the goal of AI pilot projects?
  - What are the internal capabilities related to data and AI?
  - What were the KPIs and goals for the last twelve months?
  - What are the current processes for solving the problem?

- How is performance being monitored and reported?
- How can we benchmark goals moving forward?
- What are industry benchmarks and best practices?
- What opportunities exist to create a competitive advantage?
- What technologies are being used?
  - Review current tools and processes to address the business challenge
  - Document the existing technology stack, including costs, capabilities, and utilization
- What is the structure and quality of data?
  - Document current data flow and management
  - Assess data quality and feasibility for AI applications
  - Identify opportunities to enrich and improve current data resources
  - Identify gaps in data to make recommended technologies and solutions work
  - Determine what latent assets—specifically, structured and unstructured data—can be used
  - Review the data rules, policies, standards, and models that govern data collection, storage, management, and integration
- How will the success of AI-powered solutions be measured?
  - Decide if the goal of the AI solution is focused on cost reduction, increased revenue generation/performance, or both

6. Validate issues and drivers

Does discovery research validate the initial issues and drivers? Has anything been learned that alters the issue tree and key drivers? If yes, go back to steps two and three and make the necessary changes.

Phase 2: Planning

7. Analyze options and build a solutions matrix
How can we define the path forward?

- Assess build versus buy options; determine if the organization should consider building its own solutions or buy and integrate third-party technologies
  - Identify and analyze existing third-party AI-powered solutions
  - Develop a cost and scope to build a proprietary machine-learning solution to solve the problem (if applicable)
- Ensure the solutions matrix focuses on a select group of technologies that gives your organization the ability to reduce costs through increased efficiency or improve performance through smarter technology and processes
  - Which vendors offer AI-powered solutions for the use cases?
  - How do the vendors compare on features, pricing, industry specialization, API access, customer support, product road map, funding and financial stability, integration and compatibility with existing technology stack, security, ethics policies, and more?
  - Are there options to unlock new features and capabilities within the existing marketing technology stack?
  - Which emerging AI vendors offer solutions to solve the problem?
- Note whether AI is necessary to improve processes and performance

8. Synthesize findings
What has been learned in the process? What insights will guide recommendations?

- Develop detailed strategic briefs for each vendor, including use cases it applies to, pricing, funding, customer ratings, and all information needed to secure approval and a budget for implementation

9. Develop recommendations

What actions should the organization take moving forward to address and solve the problem? How will the team monitor progress and performance?

10. Present the final report and implementation plan

What are the actions, costs, implementation timelines, and expected outcomes and ROI?

The end deliverable is a final report with key findings and recommendations. It includes an implementation plan that outlines recommended tools to address problems and details the projected road map, timelines, milestones, goals, and costs.

Following completion of the project, you will want to make sure you have the right internal and external professionals in place to support ongoing needs related to AI adoption. Solutions needed may include the following:

- Pilot Program Management: Research, plan, activate, and manage priority pilot projects
- Change Management: Educate and train staff and leadership
- Vendor Management: Evaluate vendors and manage procurement
- Development: Build custom AI solutions to fill market gaps
- Team Building: Work to build an in-house AI team
- Data Architecture: Advise on the rules, policies, standards, and models that govern data collection, storage, management, and integration
- Data Cleansing: Prepare data by detecting and correcting (or removing) corrupt, inaccurate, and irrelevant records
- Human Training: Educate personnel on new technologies and capabilities

- Machine Training: Provide the inputs and oversight needed to train AI solutions
- Integration: Integrate new technologies into existing core solutions
- Activation: Launch new solutions
- Oversight: Monitor utilization and performance, and manage vendor partnerships
- Reporting: Deliver ongoing insights and recommendations

As you can see, piloting and scaling AI goes well beyond finding a few use cases and vendors. AI will fundamentally transform your talent, technology, and strategy in the months and years to come. The organizations that take a proactive approach to investing in AI solutions and building an AI-first future will create an insurmountable competitive advantage over their peers.

Frequently Asked Questions About Getting Started with AI

Who Should Be Involved in Marketing AI Pilot Projects?

The true pioneers will involve the entire marketing team in learning and adopting AI through education, interactive training, and experiences. At minimum, you want key members of your team to be enthusiastic, rather than fearful, about the opportunities ahead and have the ability to identify use cases and business problems that AI will solve more efficiently.

What Should You Do If Your Marketing AI Pilot Project Fails?

No matter what you start with (e.g., ad spend optimization, content strategy, conversion rates, churn reduction) there is a real chance that the first couple of marketing AI pilots you run will not work, or they won't generate the cost savings or revenue growth you had hoped for. You can't stop because of early failures. That means you're going to need executive-level understanding and support of AI. The C-suite has to buy into the value and importance of transforming your marketing.

The velocity of change in marketing is going to accelerate because of AI, and it will be at a rate unlike anything we've seen before in the industry, including that of email, social media, mobile, and the internet itself. The change may appear to be gradual, but you don't want to be left behind when all of a sudden everything has evolved.

Don't try to convince executives using jargon and buzzwords. Talk to them about the metrics that matter, and show them how AI can solve real business problems in a more efficient and intelligent way. If they understand the big-picture opportunity and are engaged in the process, then early failures will be viewed as investments in the larger digital transformation.

Should AI Pilot Projects Focus on Cost Reduction or Revenue Generation?

There are two primary reasons you should consider seeking AI-powered solutions in your marketing: to reduce costs and to increase revenue. You achieve cost reduction by completing repetitive, time-intensive activities more efficiently, for example by using AI to autotag hundreds of images on your website or by applying machine learning to manage digital media ad spend. You increase revenue through more personalized and targeted marketing to existing and new customers. For example, AI can improve audience targeting as well as content and product recommendations.

For many organizations just starting with marketing AI, cost-saving use cases are likely to be the most logical for gaining early wins and executive support. However, according to an MIT Sloan Management Review and Boston Consulting Group (BCG) report, "Pioneers prioritize revenue-generating applications over cost-saving ones."[36]

So as you're building your marketing AI strategy, look for the obvious opportunities to drive efficiency and reduce costs with intelligent automation. But start developing the near-term vision for how to use AI to grow revenue through improved customer experience and identification of new markets and opportunities.

Use Cases by Marketing Category

Over the next ten chapters, we explore use cases and technology vendors by marketing category. You will find dozens of examples in the areas of advertising, analytics, communications and PR, content marketing, customer service, ecommerce, email marketing, sales, SEO, and social media marketing.

Chapter 5

Advertising and AI

Despite being a host on the Australian edition of
Shark Tank, serial entrepreneur Naomi Simson found herself in murky—
and dangerous—waters. Simson had hired multiple ad agencies to run
paid ads for her experiential gifts company RedBalloon (think Groupon
for travel and adventure excursions). The agencies claimed to know paid
advertising better than anyone, but it came at a cost. RedBalloon was
shelling out $45,000 per month on agency retainers and paying $50 or
more for each customer acquisition.

"We were being held to ransom," she said.[37]

In desperation, Simson started researching alternatives to paying an
agency to run advertising. That's how she stumbled on artificial intelligence. Simson found Albert, a company that sells an AI solution that
automatically manages and optimizes paid advertising. Intrigued, Simson had the RedBalloon team run a pilot with the solution. Her intrigue
quickly turned to amazement.

From the start, Albert did things human advertising professionals
were incapable of doing—or incapable of doing at scale. On day one,
Albert tested 6,500 variations of a Google text ad to find which one
performed best, a task that would have taken Simson's team weeks or
months. Soon after, Albert optimized every single one of the company's

ad campaigns on Facebook. Simson had set ambitious targets for the system, and it had surpassed them.

"We started out shooting for a 500 percent return on ad spend, which Albert achieved," she said.[38] Simson fired her agencies and started using Albert exclusively, supported by her team's in-house expertise.

"Now, we average 1,100 percent return on ad spend," she said. "On some campaigns, we hit 3,000 percent."[39]

The performance was stunning, but it was not the only benefit that came from using AI for advertising. Albert also found customers Simson didn't even know she had.

When analyzing RedBalloon's advertising, Albert saw something Simson and her human team hadn't. Historically, RedBalloon only advertised within Australia since its travel and adventure excursions were all local. But Albert noticed that Australians living outside the country were showing qualified interest in RedBalloon's ads. Albert experimented, and Red-Balloon's business boomed as new customers bought in droves. It turns out that Australian expatriates love to go on RedBalloon's excursions when they return home as a unique way to rediscover their country or reconnect with family and friends. Albert found this out by analyzing volumes of data that human agencies or teams just couldn't process.

"I found markets in the US and UK of people traveling to Australia that I didn't even know I had," Simson said.[40]

Simson's experience isn't unique. Today, forward-thinking B2B and B2C brands are using AI to give themselves advertising superpowers. In fact, the technology has massive implications for any company or professional that runs paid advertising through any search engine, ad exchange, or social media network.

Why Today's Advertising Runs on AI

In the heyday of Madison Avenue, consumers spent large, uninterrupted chunks of time in a few select places, such as in front of a newspaper, radio, or television, and traveling to and from work or social obligations. As a result, brands spent millions on TV, radio, and print ads designed to appeal to and capture as many eyeballs as possible to justify the money spent for a prime-time spot, front-page ad, or choice billboard. Now, millions of online destinations compete for consumer attention 24/7 across different devices and channels.

Consumers control what they read, view, and listen to and have unlimited power to "change the channel" if they aren't being served in the way they want. As a result, advertisers must compete for seconds or milliseconds of fragmented consumer attention across millions of digital destinations, apps, and experiences in real time. Advertisers are able to target consumers based on thousands of permutations of personally identifying information such as age, interests, job title, socioeconomic status, and much, much more by collecting a wealth of data on users, often through cookies (more on that in a moment). Yet manually reaching the right consumers in the right place at the right time with the right message is an impossible task for humans to accomplish at scale. That's why we now have programmatic advertising platforms, all of which depend on AI to function.

Programmatic advertising refers to the real-time buying and selling of digital ads across search engines, websites, and social networks. This is the premier way of reaching consumers today and is estimated to account for 72 percent of all digital display advertising worldwide in 2021,[41] which means AI makes possible the vast majority of the advertising you see online.

The top three companies that make money from advertising revenue—Google, Meta (Facebook), and Amazon[42]—use machine learning to serve ads programmatically to the highest bidder on their platforms second by second. Demand-side platforms and supply-side platforms also use machine learning to do the same thing for website owners, serving ads through popular services like AdRoll and Verizon Media. All platforms allow you to use increasingly granular targeting to reach segments and microsegments of select consumers moment by moment by using data collected by websites and apps through third-party cookies.

In theory, this is a major step forward for the advertising industry. AI-powered technology enables advertisers to reach more of the right people in the right moments for much less than it would have cost decades ago to buy a billboard or create a television commercial. But in practice, while the tools to target and distribute ads are decidedly futuristic, advertisers have been unable to keep up. Creating, targeting, and optimizing modern ads effectively is simply too complex a task for human advertisers to do well.

Take Meta advertising for example. Meta uses the frequency at which ads are served and how relevant those ads are to their audience as key pieces of data that inform the algorithms that price and serve their ads on Facebook and Instagram. Human experts can certainly apply their skills to optimizing against these metrics hour by hour for a handful of campaigns. But what happens if you need to run hundreds or thousands of ad variations and audience segments to truly capture enough performance to justify your ad spend? It's impossible for human teams to fully understand and execute on these metrics and others that might be influencing ad performance at scale.

You won't find ad exchanges, services, or platforms telling advertisers how their algorithms work anytime soon. The ways in which programmatic providers use AI to drive ad placements and target users is rarely revealed in full by companies eager to protect their "secret sauce." Yet behind the scenes, AI dictates whether your ads get served, how your ad budgets get used, who sees your ads, and how effective your overall campaigns are.

Use Cases for AI in Advertising

The reason marketers are turning to AI for help with advertising is simple: humans can't run complex programmatic advertising campaigns on their own or build the ad creative variations needed at scale. Sure, we're able to run campaigns across platforms like Meta, Google, and LinkedIn. But we can't cost-effectively test and optimize thousands of ads, audiences, or budget ranges, even with help from traditional software tools.

AI is here to help navigate this complexity. It can manage ad campaigns at scale and in real time and produce results humans can only dream about, which is why there are several prominent use cases for AI in advertising today.

Create Ads

AI can produce advertising copy and creative for you from scratch. Using natural language processing (NLP) and natural language generation (NLG), AI in advertising can generate hundreds or thousands of ad variations in seconds. It can also learn which ads work best from historical data, then make sure the ads it creates use those lessons to improve performance. The result is that today AI can already write some ads better than humans can.

Predict Which Ads Will Work

AI doesn't just create ads for you. It can also predict which ad text and images will work best before you even launch a campaign. It does this by evaluating the individual creative elements that work best across millions of other ads. Then it measures your ads against them and recommends what combinations of creatives will drive the best performance.

Optimize Budgets, Audiences, and Performance

AI can manage your ad budgets, audiences, and performance optimization tasks for you. Often, AI can recommend what changes to make to hit specific advertising KPIs. It can even do everything a human can do in some cases, making decisions autonomously about spend and strategy. If you're lucky, AI can even use what it learns from optimizing your ads to find new audiences for your promotions and products.

Vendors to Explore

Since 2016, we've researched hundreds of AI tools for advertising, and even piloted a few ourselves. What follows are some of the top vendors we've discovered to drive results when creating, managing, and optimizing ads.

Each is worth exploring further if you're in the market for an AI-powered advertising solution.

Albert

Albert (www.albert.ai) is AI that automatically runs and optimizes paid advertising campaigns. Albert's AI evaluates ad campaigns across Google, Facebook, Instagram, YouTube, and Bing, then makes recommendations on improving performance. The tool also automatically allocates budget, shifts targeting, and changes strategy to reach your KPIs.

Albert plugs into your existing ad tech stack, then gets to work across search, social, and programmatic platforms—covering about 90 percent of the possible biddable universe.

Celtra

Celtra (www.celtra.com) provides a creative platform that automates production to generate all the variants needed for personalized marketing. The platform has built-in intelligence for templates, including automated layouts and management of line breaks, as well as smart image cropping across any channel and format. This allows design and marketing teams to multiply creative volume and variety, go to market faster, and out-market the competition.

Pattern89

Pattern89 (www.pattern89.com) uses AI to predict which ads will work on Facebook and Instagram before you launch them. The tool evaluates billions of ads launched by brands, and figures out which colors, images, and copy work best. It then recommends how to design your ads so you can get the most clicks possible.

To do this, Pattern89 analyzes over three hundred billion data points across 49,000 creative dimensions. It then simulates variations of ads you've created to predict which will give you the best results. Today, companies like Ogilvy Social.Lab and Fabletics use the tool to create ads with a data-backed chance of performing well.

Persado

Persado (www.persado.com) uses NLP, NLG, and machine learning to help you create the right language for every ad and communications message used in every customer interaction. Advertisers can use Persado to have AI write the optimal messaging with the right emotional tone, narrative structure, level of descriptive content, and call to action. With this type of AI-powered messaging, Persado's users are able to increase conversion rates, engagement, and revenue across marketing moments.

The Death of Cookies, the Resurrection of Privacy, and the Future of AI-Powered Advertising

Cookies and the collection of user data make AI-powered programmatic advertising possible today. But what happens when it becomes harder, or impossible, to collect data on consumers?

As of the writing of this book, two major shifts in the world of consumer technology may impact the future of AI-powered advertising.

The first is the death of cookies. In 2020, Google announced it would phase out support for third-party cookies on its Chrome browser, stating that the company would not build alternative identifiers to track individuals as they browse across the web or use them in Google products.[43] Other popular browsers like Apple Safari and Mozilla Firefox already block cookie tracking, making the Google announcement the potential final nail in the coffin. This means programmatic advertisers will have far less ability to target specific consumer segments as they visit other destinations online. The ad industry is reeling as a result, with the Interactive Advertising Bureau estimating that loss of third-party cookies could lead to a $10 billion loss of revenue in the industry.[44]

The second shift is related to the death of cookies: the resurrection of user privacy concerns. Apple has announced that iOS will now prevent apps from sharing your data unless you consent to it. In the app store, apps will have to disclose how they collect and use data. On your device, apps will need to ask for your permission to use your data before collecting any information about you. Meta, which relies on this type of tracking to target ads, has come out strongly against the move. The story is still unfolding as of this writing, but the third-party cookie and user-tracking infrastructure that powers today's advertising looks to be under threat.

In the short term, it's likely going to become more difficult than it is today for advertisers to place ads in front of highly segmented audiences anywhere on the web. Advertising strategies, creatives, and budgets will need to adapt in response.

In the long term, you may end up with the ability to target and track consumers better than ever—but only with certain advertising platforms. Google, for instance, is considering a replacement for cookies called Federated Learning of Cohorts (FLoC), which would allow personalized ad targeting based on user behavior from clusters of consumers, creating privacy for individuals without sacrificing targeting capabilities. If a replacement like FLoC is used, Google would have its own proprietary way of tracking users, making the ads it sells far more valuable than those on other networks or exchanges that don't have a way to gather user data.

These sea changes in the industry mean first-party data is more important than ever. In fact, 88 percent of marketers say collecting first-party data is a priority.[45] There's a good reason for that. Without first-party data, marketers will be at the mercy of the few companies (like Google) that end up owning consumer data in a post-cookie world. To cope, marketers need to build a first-party data culture starting now, according to Mathew Sweezey, partner at the Salesforce Futures Lab.[46] This involves building a data flywheel.

A data flywheel is a constant process of data collection, usage, and enrichment. It starts by maximizing your existing technology to collect first-party data from assets you already have, then collecting more data from additional digital engagements. Data from these steps then power new data collection methods. The more data you collect, the more value and touchpoints you can provide to consumers, which are, in turn, used to collect more data.

Chapter 6

Analytics and AI

Budget Dumpster is a straightforward company. It rents dumpsters to homeowners and contractors. And it has a ton of competitors. Some competitors are small local companies in one of Budget Dumpster's markets. Other competitors are huge national firms with serious clout. Budget Dumpster's lean marketing team's job is to win business no matter who they're up against. Except the company had a problem. The analytics tools they were using didn't give them enough comprehensive intel on all the different types of competitors, and the insights their tools did surface took too long to process and use in the market.

Budget Dumpster turned to artificial intelligence to solve the problem. The company adopted AI-powered tool Crayon to inform marketing, advertising, and business strategy decisions. Crayon uses machine learning to surface insights from more than one hundred types of data across millions of sources. It then quickly provides actionable information and recommendations about what to do with that data.

In one scenario, Budget Dumpster used Crayon to brainstorm new marketing campaigns by closely monitoring what its competitors were doing online. It looked at how competitors created and promoted content, which inspired new ideas for SEO moves, landing pages to make, and social campaigns to run. In another scenario, the company analyzed the competition's gaps in online marketing and messaging. Then they swooped in to seize those opportunities.

Using this real-time approach to analytics and intelligence, the company estimates it now saves $25,000 a year on analytics activities. But it's not just about saving money; Budget Dumpster moves faster and makes more intelligent decisions thanks to AI technology. Machines collect and analyze the data, and humans hustle to execute strategies based on insights. It's a match made in heaven.

The Power of Prediction Machines

AI is so helpful in analytics because most humans aren't very good at analyzing data. Make no mistake, plenty of smart marketing pros can extract priceless insights from complex business data, but we can't extract those insights fast enough and at scale.

AI excels at analyzing large datasets, providing analytics that tell you not only what's happening now, but also what you should do about it. While you may not work for a dumpster company, you certainly deal with a lot of garbage when it comes to marketing analytics, including:

- Incomplete data to analyze
- Lack of time to properly analyze data
- Lack of resources to properly analyze data
- Insights from data that aren't useful
- Insights from data that are too slow

AI-powered analytics uses machine learning to address these issues and predict outcomes using historical data at speed and scale. And AI-powered analytics tools find patterns within large datasets, then predict future patterns using what they learned. AI is increasingly used by brands because of one simple fact: We now have too much data.

Thanks to the transition from traditional to digital marketing, we have access to web analytics through Google Analytics, marketing automation platforms, and other analytics and CMS. We have robust CRM systems and customer data platforms, and we have tons of data from promotional channels like search engines, advertising, and social media. The insights buried in this data can contain pure gold, but they require serious time and money to extract—if it's even possible to get the insights in the first place. However, today marketers have the ability to unleash AI-powered analytics across marketing organizations to extract unprecedented levels of insight.

Predictive analytics is one form of AI-powered analytics. Predictive analytics shouldn't be confused with descriptive analytics. Descriptive analytics is what we call it when we look at historical data to learn something. Standard analytics reporting is considered descriptive. Descriptive analytics activities occur manually, with human analysts interpreting results from data and analytics platforms. Predictive analytics takes this much further. It applies machine learning to the descriptive analytics data to predict what outcomes might occur in the future. The human then makes decisions based on these predictions.

Another form of AI-powered analytics is prescriptive analytics, which takes these activities to their logical conclusion. Instead of a human making decisions based on machine predictions, the machine uses its predictions to decide which actions to take. It's a natural upgrade from predictive analytics.

A predictive or prescriptive model powered by AI can take the data you already have and unlock immense value from it. AI-powered data analytics can tell you what's going right and wrong with your website, predict which leads to score as potential customers, surface insights on your competitors, and predict what your target audiences want to buy and consume. In fact, when we asked hundreds of marketers to rate their most valuable AI use cases using our AI Score for Marketers tool, many of the top-rated use cases were related to predictive and prescriptive analytics:

- Adapt audience targeting based on behavior and look-alike analysis
- Build dynamic charts and graphs to visualize performance data

- Create data-driven content
- Determine goals based on historical data and forecasted performance
- Discover insights into top-performing content and campaigns
- Forecast campaign results based on predictive analysis
- Predict content performance before deployment
- Score leads based on conversion probabilities

AI-powered analytics tools are helping marketers and brands win in three significant ways:

1. Increase revenue by analyzing and acting on data at scale
2. Reduce costs by acting on that data faster and automatically
3. Build a massive competitive advantage with both superior insights and superior speed

Are you beginning to see why AI-powered analytics is such a big deal?

Use Cases for AI in Analytics

Today, we're seeing marketers use AI-powered analytics in a few key ways to increase revenue, reduce costs, and build a competitive advantage.

Discover Insights

Human analysts can do a good job of surfacing insights from analytics platforms, but they can't do so consistently or at scale. AI, however, excels at detecting patterns in large datasets and uncovering patterns humans miss, providing a competitive edge. For instance, Google Analytics uses machine learning to answer common questions you have about your data, including why your users changed in the past week and why there were anomalies in the number of users. Google uses AI to analyze your data nearly in real time, then deliver the appropriate response.

Other AI-powered platforms do the same for proprietary business data. Some solutions, given the right data, can answer questions about business problems and make predictions about how to solve them.

Make Predictions

It stands to reason that AI systems—prediction machines—do a pretty good job of predicting. And indeed they do. Today there are AI-powered analytics systems that can analyze what your competitors are doing online, as we saw with the Crayon example. The data includes information such as product and pricing changes, personnel announcements, and content strategy. These systems then predict which of your competitors' moves matter most to you and your business, providing critical intel that can help your brand win market share.

There are also AI-powered tools that give you deep insights into your target audiences by applying sophisticated machine learning to data on online audience interests, demographics, psychographics, and behavior online and across social media. The result? Predictions about precisely what your audience wants to buy, see, and consume.

Unify Your Data

AI-powered analytics platforms can help you close the loop on all your reporting across first- and third-party sources. For instance, some AI tools can unite data from different first-party sources into a single unified customer view across channels, so you have everything in one place. From there, these tools apply machine learning to determine the likelihood of someone becoming a customer and to build more sophisticated lead segments.

AI is also being used in call tracking and analytics to connect call center sales to marketing activities. This includes using AI to close the loop on attribution across channels to dynamically routing calls between reps and teams.

Vendors to Explore

Plenty of new and existing analytics tools and platforms incorporate sophisticated AI and machine learning into their systems.

Adobe Analytics

Adobe Analytics (www.adobe.com) uses AI to analyze data from different online and offline sources, then visualizes insights from your data. Adobe's AI and machine learning come thanks to integration with the company's AI platform, Adobe Sensei. Using AI, the platform can deliver serious insights from big data at unprecedented speed.

Attention Insight

Attention Insight (www.attentioninsight.com) uses AI and proprietary data to predict how design elements will perform before they go live. Across ads, landing pages, and apps, these AI-generated attention analytics can identify issues before you spend time and money running traffic to assets.

BlueConic

BlueConic (www.blueconic.com) is a customer data platform that turns customer data into person-level profiles for marketing purposes.

BlueConic "liberates" your first-party data from all its disparate sources, then unifies it so you can use it across your marketing efforts. This results in a single customer view no matter how many analytics sources you're using. Once your data is unified, BlueConic uses machine-learning models to help you get more value out of that data, including creating customer scores and building sophisticated segmentation.

Clickvoyant

Clickvoyant (www.clickvoyant.com) is an AI-powered tool that automates the creation of analytics reporting. The tool uses NLG to dramatically reduce the time it takes to extract insights from analytics and create presentations based on those insights. It turns dozens of hours of work into minutes, refocusing human resources on value-added strategic activities.

Crayon

Crayon (www.crayon.co) is a market intelligence company that uses AI to help businesses track, analyze, and act on everything happening outside their four walls. Crayon tracks more than one hundred data types across millions of sources. It then uses AI to surface important signals for human marketers, salespeople, and analysts. The tool also recommends actions based on what it learns from the data, creating better marketing and sales outcomes.

Google Analytics

Google Analytics (analytics.google.com) is a commonly used data analytics platform that incorporates Google's machine learning to deliver insights about your data. The AI-powered advanced analytics provided by the tool are the backbone of many organizations' reporting. With Google's AI, marketers can ask common questions of their data, then receive natural language responses. The platform also uses AI to inform its smart goals, smart lists, and conversion probability capabilities.

Helixa

Helixa (www.helixa.ai) develops technology and software as a service (SaaS) products that use AI, machine learning, and other emerging technologies to combine disparate datasets and efficiently extract advanced research insights from big data. Using AI, Helixa helps produce detailed personas based on audience interests, demographics, and psychographics. That includes data on consumers at large, social media audiences, and influencers within your industry. Helixa is able to do this thanks to sophisticated AI trained on current human behavioral research and exposed to demographic and census data.

Invoca

Invoca (www.invoca.com) is an AI-powered call tracking and data analytics platform that helps marketers drive inbound calls and turn them into sales. The tool uses AI to track calls, and its analytics platform helps you connect call center sales to marketing activities in one unified view. That includes closing the loop on attribution, building audiences, and dynamically routing calls.

With Invoca, marketers can use real-time call and conversational analytics to maximize the return of their paid media campaigns in Google and Facebook, and improve the buying experience by enriching customer profiles in Salesforce and Adobe Experience Cloud.

Mobilewalla

Mobilewalla (www.mobilewalla.com) helps brands get more out of their AI investments by enriching their predictive models with third-party consumer data. The company aggregates and processes huge volumes of consumer information, then helps data scientists at brands use it to build more robust machine-learning models. That includes using third-party consumer data to build demographic and behavioral segments such as life stage, employment, interests, and many other behavioral attributes—all of which can be used by AI systems to better predict business outcomes.

How to Speed Up Adoption of AI in Analytics

As you evaluate AI-powered analytics tools, you can take a few steps to speed up your adoption process while you demo and trial technology.

1. Determine Which Metrics Matter: As you evaluate AI technology, you won't get far if your business hasn't defined which metrics matter to success. Pivoting to AI is a good excuse to get your analytics house in order, and your executives and stakeholders to agree on which key performance indicators (KPIs) matter most.

2. Evaluate Your Existing Platforms: If you use Google Analytics, you can start using AI right away, without adopting additional technology, since machine learning is baked into the platform. The same is true of certain other analytics platforms. Start experimenting with the AI capabilities offered by the platforms you already have while you build out a smarter analytics program.

3. Clean Up Your Existing Platforms: Many AI tools will draw from your existing data to make predictions. Now is a good time to make sure your organization is set up to correctly track the metrics that matter to your organization. Using a tool like Google Analytics, make sure your accounts and features (like goals and conversions) are tracking correctly to get the most value possible out of AI investments.

Chapter 7

Communications, PR, and AI

If you work in public relations or communications, your next home run could be working with a mega-influencer like Lil Miquela, a young Brazilian American woman with more than three million Instagram followers. She loves posting photos of her favorite outfits, fun travel excursions, and high-profile hangouts with celebrities and influencers. Fans comment in droves on each post about her newest look, latest musing, or most recent heartbreak. Her clout has grown so dramatically in the last few years that Lil Miquela is routinely hired by brands like Prada and Calvin Klein to promote their products. She's been interviewed as a tastemaker by *Vogue*, BuzzFeed, and The Cut, and she collaborated with MINI on an Instagram campaign to launch the automaker's latest electric vehicle.

To handle the hype, Lil Miquela signed on in 2020 with Creative Artists Agency (CAA) to represent her in commercial endorsements. CAA executive Adam Friedman told the press that the talent agency is offering "a unique opportunity for innovative, forward-thinking brands to align with a culturally relevant, icon-in-the-making."[47]

Lil Miquela wasn't present for the interview with CAA because Lil Miquela isn't real.

Make no mistake, everything we wrote above is true. But Lil Miquela isn't a person. She's an AI-powered digital avatar. She was created by a media studio called Brud, and its team engineers her every post. The crazy thing is that Lil Miquela isn't trying to fool anyone. She routinely posts tongue-in-cheek references to the fact she's a bot. Yet none of her followers seem to care. Her posts get tens of thousands of likes and hundreds of comments. Lil Miquela's team responds to comments as her and conversation ensues, just as it would with any influencer. She makes recommendations and endorsements, and her audience follows them. Quite simply, when Lil Miquela speaks, people listen. And that's all that matters to PR and communications professionals looking to turn her influence and engagement into brand equity, buzz, and revenue.

"Business is always about utility," CAA director and head of data analysis Dudley Nevill-Spencer said in the announcement of Lil Miquela's deal with the talent agency. "Miquela fills a role for a demographic, and CAA is a gatekeeper that sifts and negotiates deals on her behalf—it's that simple."

Lil Miquela is just one example of how artificial intelligence is changing the world of PR and communications. With the power of AI, brands have unlocked new ways to create and distribute their messages, protect and enhance their reputations, and inspire legions of raving fans. Today, forward-thinking brands are using AI to automatically create messages that resonate, design brand collateral tested against millions of top examples, and tap into vast dataflows that reveal consumer sentiment in real time to shape brand perceptions. And PR and communications professionals using the technology have discovered new ways to reach and influence consumers at scale. That's because AI gives you PR and communications superpowers.

PR and Communications Superpowers

PR and communications are disciplines devoted to building relationships with stakeholders and shaping the public's perception of a brand by creating strategic messages and intelligently distributing those messages to internal and external audiences. In the course of this work, PR and communications professionals tackle a huge number of tasks, including pitching publications, researching media outlets, writing press releases, crafting multimedia communications, and shaping and refining brand messaging. Many of these tasks are enhanced by technology yet are still largely manual. Even with the help of software, a human still writes and distributes releases, engages on social media, pitches outlets and influencers, builds PR and communications strategies, and reports on placements and mentions.

AI presents PR and communications professionals with an opportunity to develop a massive competitive advantage by using technology to automate, augment, and enhance what they already do, specifically making predictions and recommendations to drive business results.

Much of your work involves predicting which audiences, outlets, influencers, and messages will drive the best results for your PR or communications programs by doing things like compiling media databases, conducting outreach to audiences, and actively listening on social channels. Much of your work also involves recommending which activities have the best chance of success based on your predictions. This may include suggesting outlets and hooks for media pitches, proposing angles for messages in content and shares, and championing strategies to work with specific influencers who can reach your audience.

AI can help you do all of these things better. It can help enhance what you already do by providing greater insights and expanded data on what works with audiences, outlets, and messaging. This makes creation and distribution easier, faster, and more scalable. AI automates tedious, time-consuming tasks that take you away from the high-impact creative work you (and your bosses and your clients) love. In these ways, AI can give PR and communications professionals capabilities that turn them into bigger, better, and more powerful versions of themselves.

Use Cases for AI in PR and Communications

AI makes a long list of use cases possible for PR and communications professionals, and many more will be available in the near future as different areas of AI progress. Following are several top use cases today that we see as having the most near-term impact on the work you do in PR and communications.

Automatically Write Press Releases and Communications

NLG models like GPT-3 give PR and communications professionals the ability to generate written copy from data. In PR and communications, AI-powered tools exist that can automatically write press releases, auto-suggest language and tone changes, and even write the correct message for each customer interaction.

Create Brand Collateral

Lots of time, energy, and money go into creating eye-catching branding for internal and external content, microsites, and collateral. Each of these pieces can make or break your brand's reputation, perceived value, and equity with consumers. Not to mention, it can take weeks or months to brainstorm ideas, vet creatives, and get stakeholders to agree on impactful visuals.

Why not let AI help? AI can suggest visually appealing colors and fonts, and offer thousands of recommendations about what visual elements work well together. It can even take some of the guesswork out of design by offering suggestions and recommendations backed by millions of data points and best practices.

Detect Consumer Sentiment

It is increasingly important for PR and communications professionals to have a pulse on consumer sentiment about their brands, product categories, cultural trends, and the market as a whole. A treasure trove of data related to consumer sentiment is available through consumer-generated social media content, product reviews, comments, and user-generated web content, but it's incredibly difficult to extract insights from this data manually. This is an area where AI excels.

AI can help PR and communications professionals extract insights from social media, market intelligence, and online content in real time and at scale. These insights can then be readily used to generate brand awareness around real-time social and cultural trends, inform your next product launch, or influence your next round of communications to prospects by matching consumer sentiment extracted by AI tools.

Find (and Create) Influencers

PR and communications professionals can use AI platforms to discover the top influencers, including influencers like Lil Miquela, across the web for a particular topic and find who has the right following to promote a product or service on social media. Brands may also start creating digital avatars with their own passionate followings online to better engage with, converse with, and influence consumers.

Vendors to Explore

In communications and PR, there are a range of AI-powered tools to automate, augment, and enhance what you already do. Following are some of the vendors, ranging from startups with new cutting-edge AI tech to major established platforms that are incorporating AI into their existing products.

Beautiful.ai

Beautiful.ai (www.beautiful.ai) uses AI to design presentations with smart templates. As you add content, slides adapt to keep your presentation looking as if it were designed by a professional. Beautiful.ai also keeps the formatting and branding consistent across different presentations made by multiple team members.

Brandmark

Brandmark (www.brandmark.io) offers AI-powered design tools to create branding for collateral, even if you don't have an eye for design. The technology gives you thousands of color recommendations and finds the right font combinations. You can also create logos using AI that has been trained on over a million logos to make your next product launch or rebranding shine.

Grammarly

Grammarly (www.grammarly.com) is an AI-powered writing assistant that automatically offers suggestions for how to make your messages more accurate, effective, and impactful across emails, documents, and social media.

Grammarly is a great example of how a little AI can go a long way. Chances are people on your team are required to edit communications collateral for basic typos, language choices, tone, and clarity before it even gets into a formal review. Grammarly helps you with this, empowering individual writers to fix issues before they hit the desk of a seasoned editor. That saves the editor time and frustration, and frees them up for higher-value strategic editing and writing work.

Meltwater

Meltwater (www.meltwater.com) offers technology solutions to stream-line brand management, media relations, crisis communications, and PR reporting—and these products include AI-powered PR capabilities. As of the writing of this book, Meltwater has acquired eight AI and data-science companies to build out its AI-powered tech stack. That includes Linkflu-ence, an AI social media intelligence platform that we'll profile in chap-ter fourteen. Meltwater is one example of how established platforms are making their existing technology smarter with AI.

Talkwalker

Talkwalker (www.talkwalker.com) is an AI-powered listening and analyt-ics platform that uncovers insights from social media and online data. These insights power business decisions at thousands of brands that use the tool to uncover market data and trends in real time. The tool also helps brands keep tabs on their online reputations. Talkwalker provides an early warning system for issues related to reputational damage, so problems can be mitigated the moment they arise. It also has predictive alerts and scoring that monitor and measure your impact online.

From AI Superpowers to AI Supervillains

Today, technology enables a new form of digital engagement between a bot influencer and human audiences. It's an exciting, creative, and fun way to innovate using AI. But as we highlighted in chapter two, deepfakes can be used to harm your brand. The same goes for AI-powered influenc-ers like Lil Miquela. Tomorrow, the same or better technology could be deployed against a brand's online presence to wreak havoc. For example, Lil Miquela already has a digital rival named Bermuda, created as a stunt by the same media company. Bermuda spams Lil Miquela's profile and trashes her brand on her Instagram page.

This is all fun, games, and gimmicks, but what happens when digital influencers become so realistic or undetectable that social platform content moderators—and consumers—can't tell the difference? What is to stop a competitor from scaling up a massively popular bot influencer with the singular goal of trashing your products or services?

Thankfully, these AI supervillains aren't running amok just yet. But PR and communications professionals need to understand what's possible so we can prepare for the future. That includes becoming educated on the risks and challenges presented by the technology—so we can do our part to use these superpowers for good.

Chapter 8

Content Marketing and AI

Nobody thought a cupcake that gives advice would go viral. The Good Advice Cupcake is an Instagram account launched by media giant BuzzFeed. It's exactly what it sounds like: an animated cupcake that posts life advice. The account has more than two million followers and tens of thousands of engagements. It's so popular that Instagram contacted BuzzFeed to ask how they created such a popular account. Turns out, the answer was artificial intelligence.

BuzzFeed's data scientists and machine-learning engineers built an AI model that predicts which content stands the best chance of going viral. In the case of The Good Advice Cupcake, when the model is right, it's *really* right. And when the model is really right, BuzzFeed's bottom line benefits as traffic and ad revenue increase. The Good Advice Cupcake even has its own business line, with the Instagram account selling day planners.

But BuzzFeed isn't using AI just to create wacky content experiments. It's a truly AI-powered media company. BuzzFeed's AI experts regularly build algorithms and models that power the company's entire content machine. AI is used to optimize BuzzFeed sites, suggest content, categorize and cluster content, and create content experiments that get clicks. Some of the company's AI tools can even fully automate publishing, identify top evergreen content, and predict overall content performance across channels.

These capabilities on their own are impressive. But BuzzFeed is taking things even further. It's not just an AI-powered media company. It has actually reorganized its content business to be AI-first. Instead of just layering AI on top of existing efforts, BuzzFeed has created a content flywheel designed specifically to fuel and improve its AI systems and models.

The company uses every single publishing event as an opportunity to collect data on what drives the most engagement and revenue. This data is used to inform the next piece of content, which is iterated and improved upon based on historical data. In turn, the next piece of content generates even more data from which to learn. This data then gives BuzzFeed's AI the ability to make even better predictions about what works and what doesn't, which, you guessed it, makes subsequent pieces of content even more effective. The result is an AI-powered content machine that regularly blows the competition out of the water because it is constantly learning and improving.

This is a new way of doing content—one that uses AI from the ground up to inform content strategy, creation, promotion, and distribution. The content then informs the AI, which improves the next content efforts, creating a virtuous cycle of performance.

Forward-thinking brands and professionals have woken up to the fact that AI can power a transformative new generation of intelligent content programs. In our "2021 State of Marketing AI Report," we surveyed hundreds of marketers about their top-rated use cases for AI in marketing. Content marketing activities dominated the list. These highly rated use cases included content analysis, keyword selection, data-driven content creation, optimization, creating personalized content, and A/B testing to improve content. And, as BuzzFeed shows, these capabilities are transforming how content marketing and publishing work right now.

Why Content Marketers Must Embrace AI Before It's Too Late

Content marketers need to pay attention to AI technology. While some marketers may not believe it, AI is skilled at partially or fully producing content, promoting it, and predicting content performance. The benefits of using AI are apparent: it increases revenue by giving accurate data-driven recommendations on content that works, and it decreases costs by reducing the time, waste, and effort needed to create and promote content. That means it's a no-brainer for brands to adopt the technology to build a competitive content advantage.

AI is changing content marketing, and content marketers need to change with it. The smart move is to accept that AI-powered augmentation, automation, and disruption are inevitable. That means machines can—and will—take over some content tasks historically performed by humans. As this happens, brands will increasingly place value on humans who can do strategic and creative work.

If that describes your work today, you're in a good place. If that doesn't describe your work today—if you're primarily doing repetitive production, promotion, and scheduling tasks—your approach may need to evolve. In either event, content marketers should work toward moving up the value chain.

Content marketers can start honing the following broad skills to take advantage of AI in the coming months and years:

- AI Knowledge and Understanding: You don't need to know everything about AI to start using the technology, but it helps to have a basic understanding of the different types of AI technology.
- Data Literacy: You don't need a degree in data science to use AI to develop a competitive advantage. You do, however, need to understand basic data literacy and how data impacts AI adoption. You don't need to be a math whiz to do this, but you do need clear guidance on how to think about data and AI.

- Use Cases: You need to understand how AI can help your content marketing so you can get (and stay) ahead of the curve and begin testing tools.

With the right approach, content marketers have nothing to fear from AI. Start taking it seriously now to enhance your content marketing and give you, your brand, and your clients a competitive advantage.

Use Cases for AI in Content Marketing

Content marketing is one of the most exciting frontiers for the use of AI in the industry today. Thanks to rapid advancements in language models, next-gen content marketers are now using AI to produce more intelligent content across channels.

Create Content

NLG models like GPT-3 have ushered in a wave of AI-powered solutions that generate content. Today, AI exists that can write ad copy, snippets of blog posts, and even long-form content drafts. Using AI, brands are also automatically drafting messages personalized to each customer and addressing site visitor questions with machine-generated responses.

Optimize Content

AI excels at optimizing existing content, too. Using AI-powered platforms, brands can analyze their entire libraries of existing content and optimize every piece for maximum search visibility.

Today's AI content optimization platforms analyze more data than even a legion of content strategists could, giving you personalized difficulty and ranking recommendations to make sure you get the absolute most out of the content you already have.

Predict Content Performance

Using AI, content marketers can predict which content has a solid chance of success before they publish. It helps marketers understand which topics to write about, which topics present the most significant opportunities, and how to structure content to stand the best chance of success. AI can also identify which topics your audiences and customers care about in the first place, then suggest headlines, subject lines, and angles proven to work best with them.

Personalize and Recommend Content

AI can help you customize what your content audiences consume. By analyzing user behavior on your site, AI systems can recommend which types of content and which individual assets to serve up to users each time they return. This makes users much more likely to engage with content, stay on your site, and take conversion actions. Some AI solutions can even recommend the exact type of messaging to use so your content is personalized for specific personas, psychological profiles, and buyer types.

Vendors to Explore

With the explosion in AI advancements related to content, it's no surprise the space has plenty of compelling vendors across use cases. We've collected a handful of vendors we use to create content or have profiled to fully understand their capabilities.

Adobe Marketo Engage

Adobe Marketo Engage (www.marketo.com) is AI-powered engagement software that uses machine learning to provide content recommendations across a website. The platform uses a number of signals like engagement, CRM data, and intent to serve up the right content at the right time to every user on your site. Using Adobe Sensei, the company's platform-wide AI, Adobe Marketo Engage also learns from historical data to recommend which content is likely to perform best.

Anyword

Anyword (www.anyword.com) is an AI-powered language platform that creates content. Using proprietary data and multiple language models, Anyword generates marketing copy at the click of a button that sounds like it was written by a human. The tool leverages NLG models like GPT-3 and more than two billion data points to make content creation simple.

Copy.ai

Copy.ai (www.copy.ai) uses AI to automatically write ad copy, social media content, and website copy. Provide a short description of your copy needs, and it will autogenerate the results. You decide which copy to keep and which copy the machine should keep working on.

Descript

Descript (www.descript.com) is an AI-powered audio and video editing tool. You can use it to do traditional audio and video editing faster, or you can simply edit the text transcription it provides. You can even use its Overdub feature to create a voice-over with text-to-speech technology.

Descript also has automatic transcription and eliminates filler words from recordings with a single click.

Frase

Frase (www.frase.io) is an AI-powered engine that provides site visitors with answers to their questions using content from your website. Frase can also give you detailed analytics on which questions users are asking, then help you create content briefs around those questions so you rank higher in search results for these queries.

For content marketers, Frase offers a smarter way to both serve existing content to site visitors and help create content that drives more revenue by answering the questions users ask most.

Jasper

Jasper (www.jasper.ai) helps marketers write high-performing copy using AI. Leveraging NLG models, Jasper automatically generates different types of marketing copy. Human marketers can then select the copy they like, which trains the machine further to generate their favorite results.

Using this process, Jasper can create many different types of copy, including Amazon listings, blog post introductions and conclusions, email subject lines, Facebook ads, Google ads, Instagram photo captions, headlines, and product descriptions.

MarketMuse

MarketMuse (www.marketmuse.com) uses AI to help you research, plan, and create content better. The platform predicts content success by determining which topics to write about so you rank as high as possible, answer top customer questions, and address the most important topics for your audience. You can also order content briefs powered by AI, which contain all the information you need to create content that performs well. You can even use MarketMuse's First Draft functionality to write content for you on key topics.

Content marketers can use MarketMuse to create a smarter content strategy, optimize existing content to rank for more terms in search, and dramatically speed up and scale content marketing programs.

PathFactory

PathFactory (www.pathfactory.com) uses AI to build personalized content journeys for each person that visits your site. Using real data on visitor content consumption, PathFactory's AI will guide visitors through pieces of content that map directly to the topics they care about most. The result is that visitors engage with content more, get more value out of it, and ultimately take conversion actions based on your content.

How to Build a Smarter Content Strategy with AI

At Marketing AI Institute, we've pioneered a fifteen-step framework for building smarter content businesses and sites that we call Cognitive Content Hubs. The Cognitive Content Hub is a content engine that marries human and artificial intelligence to build an engaged audience in a centralized place and works 24/7 to grow a business. The framework, which can be applied to the launch of a new content hub or accelerating the growth of an existing blog or media site, is as follows:

1. Conduct a Market Analysis: Use LinkedIn, Facebook, Google Trends, LinkedIn Sales Navigator, and North American Industry Classification System codes to determine the size of your market. This will help you determine if a content hub is worth building and give you clues as to how much you should invest to build it.

2. Connect Content to Business Goals: Establish KPIs, including traffic, leads, and sales, to benchmark content for overall business goals. This ensures you measure and monetize your content appropriately.

3. Evaluate AI-Powered Content Tools: Using information in this chapter and online research, compile a list of possible tools to evaluate that can automate and scale content marketing. Always ask vendors how their solution is smarter than what you're doing now.

4. Identify Your Personas and Buyer Journey Stages: AI will enable highly granular targeting of micro-personas, so you don't need highly detailed personas or stages. You just need a broad definition of your target audience.

5. Create Your Content Mission Statement: Who are you creating content for? Why are you creating it? What are you creating? Distill the answers to these questions into a single sentence. Marketing AI Institute's content mission statement is "educate modern marketers on the present and future potential of artificial intelligence, and connect them with AI-powered technologies that can drive marketing performance and transform their careers."

6. Determine the Questions that Matter to Your Audience: Use tools like AnswerThePublic (www.answerthepublic.com), BuzzSumo (www.buzzsumo.com), Frase, and MarketMuse to identify the questions that matter to your audience. Complement your research with Google search autosuggestions.

7. Conduct a Content Audit: Determine which latent content assets you have that can be repurposed, updated and republished, or remixed.

8. Gather Competitive Intelligence and Market Inspiration: Leverage MarketMuse, Crayon, and Frase to brainstorm topics that matter to your audience and topics in which competitors rank. Look to your market for inspiration. Evaluate top podcasts, trade publication editorial calendars, and conference speaking topics in your space.

9. Conduct Keyword Research: Translate your core list of topics into actionable keyword research, including keyword phrases, topic clusters, difficulty levels, and search volumes.

10. Determine Editorial Focus, Formats, and Budget: Decide how your content will be differentiated from those of your competitors. What are the three to five core themes that will drive your content strategy? Commit to a core group of formats (long-form, list posts, original research, republished, curated, interviews, etc.). Pick five to seven formats, then allocate budget to production.

11. Select Your Hook(s): Every content hub needs at least one compelling hook asset to collect email addresses. These hooks can include calculators, digital books, guides, templates, and other highly valuable assets you'll give away for free.

12. Choose the Domain: Don't overthink it, but pick a domain that accurately reflects and represents your editorial focus. This may mean the obvious choice of directly integrating a blog into your company website. But putting your content hub on the main company domain isn't always the best choice when you want to build a community and movement around bigger ideas or niche markets.

13. Build the Editorial Calendar: Translate your core topics, formats, and hooks into a documented editorial calendar, preferably one that can also be built in a team project management system like Asana (www.asana.com).

14. Automate Content Reporting: Use Automated Insights or a similar automation tool to automatically produce reports based on analytics data.

15. Create the Newsletter Plan: A regular newsletter gives you the ability to build deeper relationships with your audience over time while you spin up your content production and promotion

machine. Determine the format, frequency, and technology needed to launch your newsletter, then take it live.

Check out our AI Academy for Marketers online course, *The Cognitive Content Hub: How to Build a More (Artificially) Intelligent Content Engine*, to learn more. Visit bit.ly/cognitive-content-hub.

Chapter 9

Customer Service and AI

The COVID-19 pandemic put Clorox in a tough spot. The maker of cleaning products watched its wares fly off shelves a little too fast. Stores ran out of the company's products, and Clorox couldn't restock fast enough.

The company faced a dilemma. Sales were through the roof in the short term. But with months of product shortages ahead, the brand risked fading from consumers' minds. Clorox worried that consumers would choose a new go-to brand for cleaning products when supplies came back online. The brand needed a way to create meaningful connections with consumers who couldn't buy their products or leave their homes. The solution? Clorox embraced artificial intelligence. With the help of IBM, Clorox launched a smart chatbot.

The bot used machine learning and NLP to answer questions from site visitors. It provided information on Clorox products and gave valuable tips on dealing with the pandemic. The bot was pretrained on one hundred anticipated questions from users, but it could also understand and answer many other types of queries. It debuted on Clorox's online COVID resources hub in late 2020, and that's when the magic happened.

Clorox customers and prospects engaged heavily with the chatbot. Consumers embraced the bot as a source of accurate, trustworthy advice in an environment full of misinformation. In fact, the average user had three conversations with the bot per visit. Even though there was a shortage of Clorox products available in stores, 63 percent of consumers said they were satisfied or very satisfied with their brand experience. Consumers weren't upset with the company's lack of product. They were delighted with the brand.[48]

Clorox didn't stop there. As the world reopened, the company upgraded the bot. After the pandemic, the bot provided content to help consumers navigate anxiety related to reentering the world.

Clorox's story is a glimpse into the future. Consumers no longer just want quality products at a fair price. They demand exceptional customer experiences and reward brands that deliver. In fact, consumers will pay up to 16 percent more for products or services accompanied by a fantastic customer experience, according to PwC.[49]

Brands are increasingly turning to AI to communicate one-to-one with customers at scale. They can learn more about their customers than ever before, and they can use this information to hyper personalize messages, offers, and entire experiences. Forward-thinking brands are now using AI to save significant money on customer service and experience efforts. But, like Clorox, they're also using the technology to change the game.

With AI, brands can now help every customer get what they want and need. In the process, they're changing customer service and experience from cost centers to competitive advantages.

The New Normal in Customer Service and Experience

There's no question COVID-19 changed customer service and customer experience for good. The pandemic sped up the digitization of customer interactions by three years, according to McKinsey & Company.[50] Compared to 2020, executives were three times as likely to say the majority of their brands' customer interactions are digital. This doesn't just mean brands are selling more—and more often—online. It means the entire customer journey has gone digital. Thanks to the internet, consumers have increasingly taken charge of their journeys with brands. Thanks to the pandemic, they're now entirely in the driver's seat. This new normal means consumers demand always-on, self-directed services and experiences, and failing to deliver has serious consequences.

Nearly one-third of customers say they'll stop doing business with a brand they love after *one* bad experience. After more than one bad experience, the number rises to almost 60 percent.[51] This environment has forced brands to scale digital customer service and experience. However, few brands have the resources, talent, or know-how to quickly spin up a vast 24/7 customer service and experience machine. Even if they could, they risk doing massive business damage by sacrificing the quality of service and experiences for speed and scale.

These conditions have spurred significant AI adoption in customer service and customer experience, and demand for conversational experiences is driving adoption. As a result, more customers prefer to use messaging to communicate with businesses, and brands are adapting. Of the brands that added a new service channel in 2020, 53 percent turned to messaging.[52] Clorox was one of them.

Clorox embraced AI-powered bots, conversational agents, and assistants. These tools use natural language technology to understand customer messages, then respond in humanlike ways. Conversational AI is automatic, scalable, and you can calibrate it to be empathetic and engaging to humans. So, adopting AI became a no-brainer for brands flooded with online customer requests.

But adoption hasn't stopped there. AI is driving business results elsewhere in customer service and experience, especially in back-end functions. Brands now use AI to extract insights from customer data generated by calls and messages. They use these insights to create better, more personalized experiences. Brands also deploy AI to detect content and sentiment on customer service calls, then route calls to an agent at the right time. That allows them to pinpoint the moment customers are frustrated or confused, then step in to help at the right time. They're also using AI to personalize digital experiences seamlessly. The result? AI is now accelerating revenue and reducing costs across several customer service and experience use cases.

Use Cases for AI in Customer Service and Experience

AI is being used today in a number of customer service and customer experience use cases across both customer-facing and internal functions. And, thanks to these use cases, brands are delivering more personalized digital experiences across more channels than ever.

Handle Customer Conversations

AI-powered chatbots and virtual agents are being rapidly deployed to handle customer service inquiries and user questions at scale across both text and voice platforms. Conversational AI uses NLP and NLG to understand human language and automatically create humanlike responses. When the time is right, conversational AI tools hand off customers or prospects to human agents, augmenting typical customer service and experience processes.

These tools are usually pretrained by vendors or trained on a brand's own customers and messaging data. The most sophisticated conversational agents can detect sentiment in customer messages and take actions based on customer mood, tone, and needs. Some can even recommend actions to human reps and coach them on responses if customers appear to be in heightened emotional states.

Predict Churn and Improve Experience Quality

AI can leverage your customer data in creative ways to improve service and experience. Primary among those is predicting churn and dissatisfaction. With the right data, today's AI systems can identify which customers are most likely to churn. These systems can also flag customer dissatisfaction during engagements, allowing brands to take preventative action.

AI can also extract insights from customer data that result in an improvement of the broader customer experience. By looking at past consumer behavior, AI can learn to predict future behavior and needs. These predictions are used to inform how customer service addresses questions and complaints. They're also fuel for creating a better user experience across sites, content properties, and mobile applications.

Automate Customer Service Tickets and Common Questions

Some customer service tickets, requests, and questions are simple enough for AI to handle partially or entirely. AI systems can respond to common tickets or requests automatically, freeing up human reps for higher-touch engagements. What's more, AI can handle these simple tickets and questions 24/7, leading to faster responses and fewer hours spent on repetitive tasks.

Unlock and Unify Customer Data

It's never fun getting treated like a stranger by a customer service rep at a brand you patronize often. AI can help. AI customer service and experience tools can surface relevant data about customers from CRM systems and databases when they call or chat. This gives reps immediate access to detailed information about a customer. They can then personalize conversations to deliver better service and higher-quality experiences.

Some AI tools can even unify customer data across different channels. That means you don't just unlock data about the customer's previous calls or chats. You also get up-to-date information on their behavior across all of your support channels, websites, and apps. This makes possible a level of white-glove service previously reserved only for extremely high-touch, resource-intensive support teams. It also leads to higher customer satisfaction and engagement.

Vendors to Explore

Across a number of use cases, there are several AI vendors to watch in the customer service space, including existing players and newer market entrants.

Amazon

Amazon Web Services (aws.amazon.com) is testing a sophisticated neural network–based model to automatically handle customer service requests on its site. It's also testing one to work hand-in-hand with human customer-service reps. Unlike some AI assistants that use more basic logic, the neural network–based approach holds the promise that AI will process and generate more sophisticated language and logic on its own.

Drift

Drift (www.drift.com) uses AI to power a range of conversational experiences that drive revenue acceleration. Drift's AI integrates with sales and marketing platforms to instantly engage each website visitor, personalizing the engagement based on the customer's data and historical interactions with the brand. The result is deeper conversations with prospects and customers during every step of the customer journey.

Google

As part of its Google Cloud solution, Google (cloud.google.com) offers Contact Center AI, a suite of AI tools that improve customer service and experience. The solution has AI that can understand, interact with, and talk to customers. These virtual agents are powered by the same deep learning used in Google Assistant and other Google products, and offer customer sentiment analysis to identify key decision drivers in conversations.

LivePerson

LivePerson (www.liveperson.com) offers an AI-powered conversational platform that automatically manages customer conversations across channels. The platform comes with an Intent Manager that uses natural language understanding (NLU) to identify consumer intent in conversations and then recommends actions. It even suggests conversations that can be automated further using the platform.

Microsoft

Microsoft uses AI for customer service and experience in its Dynamics 365 (dynamics.microsoft.com) enterprise resource planning (ERP) and CRM suite. Through the suite, the company offers virtual agents powered by intelligent automation to handle conversations. It also uses AI to extract insights from customer data and analytics. Its AI can even augment and enhance human productivity by delivering the right customer data at the right time to reps.

Thankful

Thankful (www.thankful.ai) is AI customer service software that uses NLP to understand and resolve customer inquiries. The tool collects relevant information about customers and advises reps on their next steps. It also personalizes messages for customers across chat, SMS, and email based on sentiment, engagement and buying history, and geography.

Zendesk

Zendesk (www.zendesk.com) offers AI-powered capabilities as part of its market-leading customer service platform. These capabilities include its Answer Bot, an AI assistant that answers common customer questions.

The platform also unifies analytics and customer data across messaging, email, chat, and voice calls.

Rising Expectations and New Pitfalls

The COVID-19 pandemic forced companies' customer service to go digital, and we're not going back. This change was fundamentally driven by consumer expectations and was a long time coming. To put it simply, we want everything better, faster, and simpler.

According to research from Zendesk, 65 percent of consumers want to buy from companies that offer quick and easy online transactions.[53] It's why 49 percent gave Amazon the best marks for service during the pandemic, and why the company is already poised to dominate the future.

Half of customers say customer service and experience is more important to them now than it was before the pandemic. Not to mention, 75 percent are actually willing to spend more on a product sold by a company with a good customer experience.

The numbers don't lie. The pandemic raised the bar for customer service and experience. Customer service is now a key strategic differentiator and necessity for every brand, and many brands are behind. Now is the time to begin using AI to catch up.

However, rising expectations also create new pitfalls. As brands move to automate and scale at speed, there's plenty of room for error. Conversational bots can make mistakes or offer unhelpful responses to hundreds or thousands of customers before someone catches an issue, which could damage your brand. Brands also need to be careful they don't remove humans entirely from the process. Just because consumers want speed doesn't mean they want to sacrifice a human touch and empathy. This makes AI-powered customer service a necessity but also a balancing act. Brands need to get both the hardware and the heart behind great customer service right.

Chapter 10

Ecommerce and AI

Pomelo Fashion is an ecommerce fashion company that sells apparel in Southeast Asia. With more than $80 million in funding, the company wanted to make significant growth investments. Artificial intelligence was a top priority.

Pomelo already had an AI algorithm that recommended products to site users. But the algorithm wasn't helpful anymore. It used old data, had limited inputs, and wasn't very good at personalization. The algorithm used product page ranks and other general data points to suggest new wares. It treated every customer the same, not taking into account individual preferences or behaviors.

The company knew all too well how hard it would be to rebuild its AI from the ground up. It would need to build new models and use new data sources. As the world went online during the COVID-19 pandemic, Pomelo wasn't sure if it had the luxury to launch a multiyear machine-learning project.

To help, it turned to the best in the ecommerce business: Amazon. Amazon doesn't just use AI for its own product recommendations. It also sells a machine-learning service called Amazon Personalize through its AWS arm. With Personalize, Amazon helps other firms adopt its sophisticated product recommendation AI. Amazon's system is proven, it's primarily prebuilt, and it's easy to deploy. To use it, Pomelo didn't need to start from scratch.

Using Amazon Personalize, Pomelo got a 400 percent ROI within a month. The brand quickly deployed it across other areas of the site. In the company's dresses category, more intelligent recommendations boosted revenue by more than 18 percent.[54]

Pomelo's story doesn't just prove the power of AI in ecommerce. It also points to the sea change happening in ecommerce. It's a transformation that has made AI a business necessity and has positioned one company to rule the industry and its use of AI.

Amazon and AI

Ecommerce was already eating the business world before COVID-19, but the pandemic poured gasoline on the fire. In 2020 alone, ecommerce transactions jumped a whopping 30 percent as consumers went all-in shopping online.[55] In fact, research from Shopify estimates that ten years of ecommerce growth happened in just ninety days in 2020.[56] Brands had to meet consumers on their own turf. Everything, including marketing, support, and supply chain had to change almost overnight to be digital and ecommerce-first.

As a survival mechanism, ecommerce marketers embraced AI-powered technology. Conversational agents and bots became essential to handle sales and support. Recommendation and discovery were critical to generate sales during entirely self-directed customer journeys. And forecasting was mandatory to stay stocked amid unprecedented demand.

Amazon was already there. In 2003, Amazon researchers published a seminal paper on AI that used collaborative filtering to create product recommendations. The researchers discovered that they could make accurate and helpful product recommendations based on the preferences of all shoppers, not just one. The technology soon formed the core of Amazon's legendary product recommendations. As far back as 2014, AI product recommendations accounted for 35 percent of all Amazon sales.[57]

The company has come a long way since then. Today, it uses AI across a considerable number of business lines and use cases. Many of these are directly revolutionizing ecommerce as we know it.

Behind the scenes, Amazon uses highly sophisticated robots to automate activities at its warehouses and fulfillment centers. These robots pair with advanced machine-learning systems to orchestrate and optimize robot and human activities. In fact, AI is critical to keeping Amazon's market-leading logistics machine competitive.

Amazon has also used AI to transform consumer-facing applications and buying experiences. Its development of a leading voice assistant (Alexa) has created a brand-new purchasing channel for consumers and new ecommerce revenue streams for the company.

Amazon is also unlocking AI capabilities for other ecommerce brands. AWS incorporates prebuilt machine-learning models that recommend and personalize products for brands. These models offer predictive capabilities and are available to any brand using Amazon's Personalize service.

Amazon possesses a potentially insurmountable advantage in AI for ecommerce. It has some of the best algorithms, talent, computing power—thanks to AWS and massive investments in computing infrastructure—and more data on consumer purchases and habits than almost any other company on Earth. Early AI adoption has created a flywheel effect at Amazon. The smarter its AI gets, the more it sells. The more it sells, the more data it collects. The more data it collects, the smarter its AI gets.

Amazon doesn't just have a head start when it comes to AI for ecommerce. It's running an entirely different race by dominating both ecommerce and the source layer for AI technology in ecommerce. As more ecommerce companies adopt AI out of necessity, they're not just trying to be—or beat—Amazon. They're actually reliant on AI from Amazon to compete in the first place.

Use Cases for AI in Ecommerce

Thanks to companies like Amazon, AI is everywhere in ecommerce. Today, it accelerates revenue and reduces costs across several use cases.

Fulfillment, Inventory Management, and Demand Forecasting

More companies are adopting robotics powered by AI to automate warehouse and inventory tasks. Major ecommerce players like Amazon use AI-powered robotics to sort items and pack orders automatically. AI directs human workers, charting the optimal actions to maximize efficiency and speed.

AI is also used to manage inventory. By using advanced predictive models, companies can better regulate stock and anticipate buying patterns. That allows top ecommerce players to deliver on a promise of one- or two-day shipping. It controls costs by avoiding downtime or misallocation of warehouse space, and it prevents product shortages by using warehouse data to forecast demand better.

Personalized Product Recommendations

Personalized product recommendations are a significant use case for AI in ecommerce. Using customer data, brands can use AI models to predict which product consumers will want to buy next. Suggesting the right product to the right consumer increases overall purchases, repeat purchases, and average order size. It also generates more data to help AI systems improve their recommendations in the future.

AI can make recommendations across a customer base. By looking at what specific customers buy, AI recommenders can find patterns and make predictions about what other customers may want. Brands can apply this technology across different types of purchases, trends, and conditions, such as seasonality.

Virtual Try-On

As consumers steadily replace in-person shopping experiences with ecommerce, brands are deploying AI to mimic certain in-store experiences at home. Chief among these are virtual try-on experiences, where consumers can simulate how different products look on them. Virtual try-on relies on image recognition and computer vision to accurately show consumers how clothes and accessories will look on them. AI-powered try-ons can also include virtual fitting functionality to reliably size clothing from home.

Another version of this is visual previews deployed by some brands that sell large products like furniture. Using the same types of AI technology, visual previews help at-home shoppers envision precisely how a piece of furniture or other large item will look in actual rooms.

Product Search and Discovery

AI makes more intelligent product searches and discoveries possible across text, voice, and visual searches on ecommerce websites. AI can understand site search queries, then return the appropriate products in written or audio formats. It can also recognize and deliver accurate image-based results of products that match specific visual features.

Predictive Product Development and Pricing

The most sophisticated AI can predict which products to develop and how to price new or existing offers. By analyzing consumer preferences, AI systems can pinpoint which features and functionality existing customers demand. They can also identify broader consumer preferences across markets by analyzing reviews, trends, and sentiment across channels like social media. Brands can then use this information to develop new ecommerce products or expand existing product lines.

Brands also use AI to inform pricing in various ways. AI systems can determine the optimal pricing for each product using customer and ecommerce data or by optimizing pricing for individual customers based on their preferences and needs.

Vendors to Explore

Given how much buying now happens online, many vendors offer robust AI solutions to provide better product recommendations and personalized experiences across ecommerce stores.

Amazon

Amazon (www.amazon.com) offers its Amazon Personalize machine-learning service to ecommerce companies through AWS. Using Personalize, brands can create AI-powered recommendations, build smarter upsells and cross-sells, and incorporate intelligent product discovery features into their sites.

BigCommerce

BigCommerce (www.bigcommerce.com) offers an ecommerce platform designed to scale through storefront design and conversion capabilities. As part of those capabilities, the platform's app store has a number of integrations with AI-powered apps. These apps offer functionality around personalization of content and products, as well as audience segmentation and recommendation.

Klevu

Klevu (www.klevu.com) is an AI-powered ecommerce search solution that uses NLP and machine learning to assess customer searches and deliver product recommendations. This helps consumers find exactly what they're looking for and helps them uncover things they never knew they wanted, boosting ecommerce revenue.

NLP helps Klevu extract more meaning and context from search queries and match more terms to results that other technologies are unable to match. Klevu also uses machine learning to promote products based on how users are interacting with them, providing more real-time promotion of items based on their popularity and effectiveness. The key interactions that Klevu uses are completed purchases, adds to cart, and clicks. These actions give users an understanding of product popularity.

Qubit

Qubit (www.qubit.com) helps brands create AI-powered ecommerce experiences. The tool offers product recommendations powered by machine learning, as well as personalized content recommendations and product discovery. It also uses predictive and affinity-based algorithms to make predictions based on customer behavioral data. Qubit even connects to all your other data sources so you can apply AI to your existing data from other platforms.

Shopify

Shopify (www.shopify.com) has a multitude of AI apps that plug into its ecommerce platform. Using these AI capabilities, Shopify users can deploy machine-learning models across the buying cycle, optimizing for everything from reducing cart abandonments to limiting user churn. AI can also be used for user segmentation and customer insights. There are even AI apps that will do your Shopify store SEO for you.

Zoovu

Zoovu (www.zoovu.com) is an AI-powered conversational search platform that uses NLP to drive sales conversations between ecommerce companies and their customers. The company's AI not only engages with customers but also learns their behaviors and preferences.

Zoovu uses NLG to drive both structured and unstructured conversations between digital commerce companies and their customers. Using machine learning and a training database of billions of buyer interactions with over five hundred product categories, Zoovu can help customers find what they are really looking for using natural language instead of technical jargon and specs.

To Buy or to Build?

The story of Pomelo Fashion at the beginning of this chapter illustrates a classic conundrum facing companies that are exploring AI for ecommerce: whether to buy an AI system or to build one.

Every organization and use case is different, so you'll ultimately need to answer this question for yourself. But a few strong arguments can be made for buying the technology you need in ecommerce rather than building an AI system yourself.

- The Speed of Ecommerce: Ecommerce moves so fast that building AI from scratch may leave your company perilously exposed as competitors move faster to implement smart AI-powered capabilities.
- The Availability of Powerful Technology: Thanks to Amazon and other major platforms (BigCommerce, Shopify), ecommerce companies have ready access to powerful AI that some other sectors just don't have yet. Today, you can buy robust out-of-the-box AI to handle product recommendations and personalization.
- The Immediate ROI: Other sectors and use cases may take time to see a return on AI investments. However, ecommerce companies can often pay for the technology quickly since it should directly translate into sales if it works and is applied appropriately.

Chapter 11

Email Marketing and AI

Matt Moscona hosts a sports radio talk show on ESPN 104.5 out of Baton Rouge, Louisiana. His fans love him, but they're always hungry for fresh content. So Moscona started a daily email newsletter to further engage with his audience. He had a problem, though. Email marketing is hard. Really hard.

Moscona spent hours each day hunting down compelling content for the newsletter. It was eating up much of his day, and he never knew which content would land with his audience. After all, everyone has their own preferences. Some fans obsessively follow home teams. Others only care about a single sport. How do you cater to every single person's preferences in one general email?

To solve the problem, Moscona turned to artificial intelligence. He used a tool called rasa.io to build a truly personalized email newsletter using machine learning. First, Moscona entered a series of popular content sources into the tool. Then rasa.io automatically pulled links from each source to create a newsletter. Every time a reader clicked on a link, rasa.io learned their preferences, then customized their newsletter to those preferences on the next send. As a result, each reader got an individual newsletter wholly customized to their particular interests. Moscona still added his own personal touch to each newsletter, but the AI handled the automation and personalization at scale.

Smarter email marketing gets results. Moscona's open rates shot up to 50 percent because the email newsletter served readers with hyper personalized content. Now Moscona focuses his time and energy on creating incredible content for his audience.

AI hasn't put him out of a job. AI empowered him to build a deeper connection with his audience, and it freed him to do more of the work he loves. It's a win-win relationship. Brands can use AI to create scalable machine-driven email campaigns that get results. Email marketers get to do more of the creative, strategic work they love. Those are just a couple of the reasons email marketing is quickly becoming a top area where marketers and machines work hand-in-hand.

Humans Plus Machines Equals Email Marketing Success

Moscona's story shows why email marketers are turning to AI. We listen to our guts too much. It's understandable since a gut feeling is an essential human function. It's the sensation from deep within our lizard brains that tells us something feels right or wrong. It's helpful out in the wild, but when it comes to email marketing, our guts are usually dead wrong.

We're bad at predicting which emails other humans will find engaging. We use guesswork to determine which emails to send. We rely on personal preference to decide what content goes in those emails. We don't even agree with each other half the time about email strategy. The sad truth is that we still rely too much on conjecture to choose subject lines, plan email content, pick send times, segment lists, and structure calls to action. We pray for miracles and hope for magic. That's never been more dangerous, and the math proves it.

In 2019 alone, users sent 293 billion emails per day. In 2022, that number is projected to be 347 billion per day.[58] More than a third of marketers send customers three to five emails per week. The sheer volume of emails makes consumers discerning, with almost half of consumers saying they decide to open emails based on the subject line alone. Email clients use sophisticated algorithms to block and sort communications, in part to deal with the 14.5 billion spam emails every day. A full 16 percent of emails are estimated never even to make it to their recipients.

It has never been more important to stand out in the inbox. More than half of consumers buy something at least once a month following a marketing email in the B2C world. Almost 60 percent of B2B marketers say email is their top revenue-generation channel.[59]

Email marketing is just too important to leave to chance. That's where AI comes in. Today, AI isn't just for writing subject lines, though it's excellent at that. It can evaluate your database to make sure it's healthy and valid. It can use email validation to make sure you actually land in someone's inbox. And it can help you segment lists better, so you deliver more relevant offers to your valuable customers. That's because AI handles a complexity that we can't.

Human marketers can't monitor and react to algorithmic changes in the filters used by email clients. We can't efficiently clean up lists so that our emails go to the right people, especially in large databases. We can't do advanced list segmentation. We can't even consistently create email copy that customers and prospects love. It's not because we're bad at marketing. It's because we don't have the capacity for analysis, pattern recognition, and forecasting that AI can achieve at scale.

In this way, AI presents an opportunity, not a threat. When it comes to email marketing, the technology does what we can't, handles everything we're bad at, and lets us focus on our strengths.

Use Cases for AI in Email Marketing

AI is an email marketer's new best friend. It can make sense of your data, so you can base campaign decisions on math. It can optimize your campaigns and put more money in your pocket. In some cases, it can even contact prospects for you.

Manage Email Conversations with Prospects

Thanks to NLP and NLG, AI can have email conversations with your prospects, qualify leads by email, and automatically book meetings. AI will send an email to a prospect, then use its language abilities to manage a conversation until it's time for a rep to take over. It can even draft responses to prospects and predict when they should receive a more human touch.

With AI, reps don't have to manually contact, respond to, or qualify early-stage prospects by email. Instead, they can focus on higher-value nurturing and sales conversations. It's a better way of doing email communication, one that allows you to scale without hiring more people.

Clean and Enrich Contact Records

Keeping contact databases clean and accurate is a massive task for human teams, especially when databases grow large. That's why brands increasingly turn to AI-powered tools for help.

AI can ensure that contact information in your database is accurate, consistent, and deduplicated. It can also enrich contacts by contextually extracting accurate data from email conversations. That makes email list maintenance much, much easier for humans.

Write High-Performing Email Subject Lines

AI has the power to analyze your human-written copy and then write email subject lines that perform better than ones written by people. Today, AI can analyze the emails you've sent, then extract your brand tone and determine what language works best. It can then automatically write thousands of subject lines and find which ones perform well. The best part? AI tools for writing subject lines learn and improve after each email your customers open and respond to, making future efforts even more successful.

Optimize Send Times

If you give AI access to your CRM and marketing automation systems, it can tell you when the best time is to send an email, and it can do so for every single contact in your system. AI finds patterns in each individual's engagement with past emails. It then uses those patterns to predict when the prospect is most likely to open your next email. AI will then handle sending each email at a time explicitly customized to the prospect receiving it. The result is higher open rates and more engagement because every person on your list receives your email at the best time for them.

Segment Contacts Based on Behavior

Savvy email marketers know the value of segmented lists. Segmented email campaigns have been shown to increase revenue by 760 percent.[60] But that segmentation can be based on infinite criteria. So how do you know you're spending valuable time segmenting for the most impact?

Smart segmentation with AI is a great place to start because it will help you develop lists that increase opens and clicks. AI can surface insights from your contacts that you can use to better segment based on behavior. For instance, AI can tell you which groups are most likely to engage with your emails or take action on an offer. Using this information, you can create more valuable lead segments to drive email performance. AI can even discover signals your strategists miss, thanks to its ability to detect patterns hidden in large datasets.

Vendors to Explore

Most brands have an email database with common data on clicks, opens, and engagement times, providing a wealth of data for AI tools. That's why there are plenty of robust AI products for email marketing. Following are several top vendors we have demoed or actively use for Marketing AI Institute's email marketing.

Phrasee

Phrasee (www.phrasee.co) uses advanced AI to automatically write email subject lines better than humans, resulting in higher open rates. The solution assesses the copy your human copywriters have written to learn your brand voice, then uses NLG to write a large number of email subject lines that are designed to achieve your performance goals.

The solution writes email subject lines so well that Phrasee claims it beats humans in 98 percent of head-to-head tests, producing copy that gets more opens, clicks, and conversions.

rasa.io

rasa.io (www.rasa.io) sends personalized smart newsletters tailored to each prospect's individual content preferences. Using AI, rasa.io evaluates how each user engages with content in your email newsletter. Then it customizes future newsletters to deliver more of the content an individual prefers, making it more likely they'll engage with your email.

Using rasa.io, brands can automatically nurture their email lists with value-driven content personalized on a one-to-one basis, resulting in more opens, clicks, engagement, and sales from email.

Seventh Sense

Seventh Sense (www.theseventhsense.com) optimizes the time of every email you send so it reaches a prospect's inbox at the moment they are most likely to open and click on the email. Seventh Sense's AI assesses mountains of user data from your HubSpot, Marketo, or corporate email portals, then predicts the optimal time each user engages with email across your entire database. Seventh Sense will even help you predict with accuracy which audience segments are most likely to open your next email.

Building a More Intelligent Email Marketing Machine

There's no question that AI can improve your email campaigns. But how do you get started building a more intelligent email marketing machine? It all begins with identifying the problems you have with your email marketing, then exploring use cases to solve those problems. What issues plague your email campaigns? What technology can help? To get you started, here are the issues we see email marketers run into again and again:

- Bad lists
- Deliverability issues
- Difficulty predicting campaign success
- Low click rates
- Low open rates
- Poor engagement
- Poorly segmented lists

You don't need a PhD to discover and use AI solutions. You need a list of problems to solve and the curiosity to research further. There's a decent chance your problems are related to human limitations, a good chance technology exists to help, and a great chance that AI powers that technology.

Chapter 12

Sales and AI

You hear a lot of doom and gloom about how machines are coming for everyone's jobs. But the sales team at Okta are pretty happy they turned things over to our robot "overlords."

Okta is a publicly traded company that helps customers secure employee identities. With a $33 billion market cap and more than ten thousand customers as of December 2021, Okta is growing like crazy. That growth presented its sales team with new opportunities—and new challenges.

As the company scaled, the sales team struggled to give each and every prospect a fully personalized experience with Okta. As a result, it was missing out on deals. That's why Okta turned to an artificial intelligence solution from Drift, a tech leader with $107 million in funding. Drift's revenue acceleration platform uses AI to qualify, nurture, and help close more sales leads. It does this by automatically prioritizing target accounts, centralizing sales insights, and personalizing outreach using the power of sophisticated machine learning.

Far from replacing Okta's sales team, Drift's AI became the team's newest rock-star colleague. Using Drift, Okta's team increased influenced pipeline by 30 percent quarter over quarter in the first six quarters. The team also doubled the conversion rate from marketing qualified lead

(MQL) to sales qualified lead (SQL) using AI. Not to mention, AI became the fastest channel that converted MQLs to pipelines. This is because AI fills critical gaps in sales operations.

Drift's AI, for instance, helps automatically determine that prospects are far enough along in the funnel before sending them to business development representatives and sales development representatives. It also vets leads to see if they have enough knowledge about the product to make a sales conversation worthwhile. It's as if Okta has a clone army of sales associates that don't sleep and know exactly how to talk to prospects.

For Okta, AI isn't an overhyped buzzword. It's not a magic technology being sold as a one-size-fits-all solution. And it's certainly not some terrifying indicator that layoffs are coming and salespeople are obsolete. AI is a practical tool and career game changer for every single salesperson at Okta. It doesn't just put more money in their pockets—it puts them miles ahead of the competition.

Why Salespeople Need AI

Most salespeople stop paying attention when someone mentions AI, and it's understandable. Salespeople know that truly effective sales work can't be done by machines, and they're skeptical of anyone who says otherwise. This misses the point. AI in sales isn't about replacing seasoned salespeople at all. As Okta's use of AI shows, AI is about helping seasoned salespeople sell more. Much, much more.

Consider how much time you and your team spend on activities that don't involve closing deals. We're talking about building pipelines, prioritizing leads, sourcing new deals, hunting down contact information, booking meetings, keeping CRM records updated, researching and profiling prospects, and a hundred other activities that require time, energy, and focus. AI can help you automate or augment most of these tasks so you can focus on your quota. It can also help you do mission-critical tasks much better and at scale, which helps you hit that quota—or even crush it—faster. That's because AI excels at taking your sales data and using it to make better predictions and recommendations than humans alone can.

Whereas traditional software uses simple rules-based automation to streamline your work, AI actually finds insights, opportunities, and patterns that traditional software can't. AI can detect churn signals in real time, predict which leads will close, and find new leads that match your ideal prospects.

At the end of the day, AI isn't a magic wand. It's a smarter solution than the ones most salespeople use today. It creates practical value for sales teams by automating, augmenting, and supercharging the way they work better than anything else available.

Next-gen brands are catching on to this fact. Sales leaders polled by Salesforce expect their AI adoption to grow faster than any other technology adoption.[61] In fact, Salesforce found that high-performing teams were almost five times more likely to be using AI than underperforming ones.

Use Cases for AI in Sales

Sales is one of the biggest areas where AI can have an impact. That's because sales teams have a big problem. While most organizations have a treasure trove of data they should be using to drive smarter sales outcomes, their teams have little time or bandwidth to effectively use this data in their work.

AI for sales can help you sell more by using your data to make predictions and recommendations that close more deals, and it can help you spend less by automating manual tasks and making your sales teams more productive.

Forecast Sales Outcomes

When we judge which leads will close in any given quarter, we're making a prediction about a future sales outcome. AI can make these predictions with much greater accuracy than we can. AI uses data on lead engagement, conversions, closed-won deals, closed-lost deals, and many other events to accurately forecast sales outcomes. Those outcomes can include forecasting who is most likely to close and who to target next—and that's just within your existing pipeline. AI can also find new prospects that are most likely to close from pools of leads that are not currently in your system.

AI-powered forecasting creates value for sales teams internally. Using predictions about who is likely to close and when, sales managers can forecast their teams' performance in advance and take proactive steps to hit quotas.

Score Leads

Humans approach lead scoring in an unscientific way. We use gut instinct and incomplete information to form judgments about leads. At best, human-led lead scoring is imperfect. It surfaces some useful leads but fails to find every lead of value and often prioritizes plenty of bad leads in the process. At worst, human-led lead scoring is just plain wrong and creates more work for sales.

AI has the ability to look at all the relevant data, then score leads effectively and consistently. It can evaluate data that humans don't have the time, ability, or bandwidth to evaluate themselves. AI can look at the entirety of a prospect's historical information, social media presence, and past engagements with sales to arrive at a more informed lead score.

AI takes the same approach to lead scoring that humans do. It evaluates data related to your leads, then prioritizes those leads based on data that signals fit and intent. It just does it better, faster, and smarter than you ever could—and it does it at scale.

Qualify Leads

This problem may sound familiar. You have MQLs coming in but not enough hours in the day to follow up, nurture, and qualify these leads for further sales conversations. It's a good problem to have, but a problem nonetheless. And it's a costly one. You're leaving money on the table every time you fail to adequately follow up with (and qualify) a warm lead.

That's why brands are using AI for lead qualification. AI exists today that can have conversations with leads for you through email, chat, and SMS. These AI sales assistants reach out to every new lead, check if they have questions, ask qualifying questions, book meetings, and navigate scheduling. When the time is right, they hand off conversations to human reps.

AI makes it possible and cost-effective for teams to qualify every lead in their pipelines without growing head count.

Recommend Sales Actions

Some AI tools will actually tell you which actions make the most sense based on an analysis of your available data. Once AI makes predictions about sales performance, it can advise you on how to price a deal, who to target next, or how to best target specific customers with upsells or cross-sells. This frees salespeople to structure the perfect offer and close more deals instead of wasting time deliberating about what to do next.

Enhance Productivity

It's no secret that sales requires a lot of manual labor and grunt work. Some of this effort is just the price you pay to close deals and win markets, but many of the tasks you do daily are mundane, manual, and unnecessary.

AI offers several opportunities to automate or augment time-consuming sales work that distracts you from high-value, high-impact tasks. AI exists today that can book your calls, schedule meetings, recommend recurring events and follow-ups, and manage calendars. It can automate standard email responses and even evaluate if leads are worth talking to in the first place. Chances are, if you spend time manually doing specific activities over and over, AI can make those activities easier and faster, or take them off your plate entirely.

Vendors to Explore

AI vendors for sales range from innovative, fast-growing startups to established companies that have injected AI into their product lines. Here are several vendors worth a look if you're interested in deploying sales AI.

Drift

Drift (www.drift.com) uses AI in its revenue acceleration platform to deliver personalized customer experiences to each and every prospect across all your channels. Sales teams use Drift to automatically qualify prospects, have more productive sales conversations, and accelerate time to close.

Exceed

Exceed (www.exceed.ai) uses AI to understand conversations and engage with leads, driving more pipeline by ensuring each lead is qualified and nurtured. The platform's conversational marketing assistant then automatically books meetings on your reps' calendars when a lead is qualified enough. The tool acts as a multiplier for sales reps, enabling them to have conversations with leads at scale without you needing to add more reps.

Gong

Gong (www.gong.io) captures all of your sales conversations, including phone calls and emails, then uses AI to analyze what makes these conversations successful. This intelligence empowers sales to identify deal churn signals, replicate what the best sales reps do to close, and coach reps on how to close more.

HubSpot

HubSpot (www.hubspot.com) has a number of AI-powered features as part of its Sales Hub product. Those features include AI that deduplicates contact records and cleans up databases, as well as automates sales call transcriptions and email data captures, and has live chat name recognition capabilities. You can even use HubSpot's AI to scan business cards and automatically detect first name, last name, email, and other information, then create and update CRM records automatically.

MadKudu

MadKudu (www.madkudu.com) is an AI-powered marketing intelligence platform that helps marketers build models to better score, prioritize, and understand leads and accounts. The platform also uses machine learning to help you identify leads that are a good fit and make predictions about how much they'll spend.

Rev

Rev (www.getrev.ai) uses an AI-powered predictive model to find B2B audiences that look like your best or ideal customers. The model improves over time, helping sales reps build pipelines with qualified companies that are a great fit for their products or services.

Salesforce

One of the top players in AI for sales is Salesforce (www.salesforce.com). The company's AI is called Einstein, and it shows up in many places throughout Salesforce's platform. Einstein automatically prioritizes leads for your sales reps, evaluates the likelihood of deals that will close, and empowers developers to bake AI into their Salesforce apps.

Einstein is integrated into Salesforce's main products, as well as into acquired platforms like Pardot (www.pardot.com), a leading marketing automation solution. With Einstein, Pardot users can leverage AI-powered lead scoring and behavior scoring to accurately predict when leads are ready to buy.

How to Enable Your Sales Team with AI

If you're convinced AI for sales is worth a look, then the next step is to get sales teams on board. How do you convince colleagues and bosses that AI is a good idea? And how do you enable sales to understand, value, and adopt AI—either as a member of the sales team or an outside marketing champion? There are three steps you can take to start enabling sales teams with AI.

1) Think Like Sales

Getting sales teams on board with AI just means you're selling AI internally. Like any good sales process, you need to know your prospects.

If you're on the sales team, you already have a good idea of what your colleagues do and don't care about in their work. Any conversation about AI needs to start by directly relating to a sales team's biggest challenges, or it's a nonstarter. Pitch AI as a tool to book more meetings, calls, or demos and close more deals, then go from there.

If you're a marketer enabling sales with AI, you need to know that salespeople are different from you. Salespeople care about the bottom of the funnel, not the top or middle like you do. They want buyers, not users, fans, or audience members like you do. They're obsessed with moving people through their pipelines; they don't care about how AI helps you get more traffic, leads, or engagements. They care about how AI makes it easier for them to close and hit quotas. No matter where you are on the organizational chart, think like sales if you want to effectively sell AI to them.

2) Do the Work for Them

Don't expect anyone to do a lot of homework unprompted. Once you pitch AI as a solution, you should accompany that pitch with concrete AI use cases and tools for sales. It's not enough to cite statistics or talk about broad business trends. You need to bring examples to the table. This chapter offers several examples to use. You can also do your own research and start mapping AI vendors to different sales stages in the sales process. This approach gives sales teams a clear picture of exactly how AI can fit into their existing workflows, which makes the value of AI clear and reduces fear that it requires a lot of change.

3) Serve Them the Content They Need

After an initial conversation about AI, treat salespeople like any other prospect: continue to nurture them with relevant, helpful content to continue the conversation. Elements of this chapter make for a useful initial follow-up, giving sales professionals the information they need to investigate use cases and vendor names on their own.

You may also want to direct sales to helpful articles online about their particular challenges and how AI can help.

Chapter 13

SEO and AI

It's no easy feat to grow a brand's organic traffic by a factor of fifteen. It's even harder to do that in less than six months. And it seems downright impossible to do it when your core audiences span a variety of business functions, including marketing, sales, and project management. That is unless you have artificial intelligence on your side.

Monday.com, a project management platform, knows this all too well. The company used AI to increase search traffic by a stunning 1,570 percent over just a few months. Monday.com scored dozens of page-one search results and increased its ranking position by an average of twenty-five positions on Google for each keyword being tracked.[62] (This is all despite being in a popular, crowded market.)

Previously, the company relied on manual keyword research and SEO briefs. The process produced high-quality content, but it was time-consuming. In some cases, it leaned on paid advertising to bring in traffic. The company needed a smarter approach, one that generated traffic cost-effectively, sustainably, and at scale. So, it turned to an AI tool called MarketMuse.

MarketMuse uses AI to optimize content for searches, but unlike traditional SEO software, it doesn't give you generic keyword research and ranking information. It shows you SEO opportunities based on a personalized difficulty score that is unique to your site. The tool then recommends which topics to attack based on these scores and builds briefs that show you exactly how to write content that ranks.

MarketMuse showed Monday.com exactly what topics to target and what opportunities to prioritize. It even provided a brief for each topic that showed the company exactly how to rank for it. As a result, Monday .com was able to both optimize existing content and scale up content creation. In the course of several months, the company handed off Market-Muse briefs (based on AI-powered SEO research) to outside writers, who were able to produce high-quality content quickly. Instead of paying for advertising or doing everything manually, Monday.com ramped up a process-driven content machine that eventually produced one hundred search-optimized articles per month.

The results spoke for themselves. Monday.com's organic traffic and search rankings exploded, and the company's traffic became fully sustainable without additional advertising spend. It's an SEO success story that simply wouldn't be possible without AI.

Search engines now use advanced algorithms to serve consumers the most relevant search results across devices, employ machine learning and NLP to predict search intent and match results to it, and take into account user behaviors and interactions across text and voice. Gone are the days of writing content to match simple keywords.

Today's search environment is a complex combination of platforms dominated by algorithms and AI. These machines reward much more than just including a specific word or phrase. When making judgments, they evaluate all your content and the context around it. What they reward and penalize changes frequently, often with devastating results for unprepared brands. And they make decisions about search results second by second, 24/7, at scale, using billions of pieces of data.

Manual keyword analysis and guesswork just don't cut it anymore. Monday.com discovered that the hard way, but it also found the way forward.

AI tools for SEO give brands an extraordinary ability to survive and thrive in today's search environment. They make it possible to pull back the curtain on what works in search—analyzing large datasets in ways that humans can't—and they offer the speed and scale that is required to keep up with search powered by machines.

Why AI Is Essential for SEO

Every search engine in existence has a single goal: to serve you the perfect answer for your query. It's the same goal search engines have always had, but the ways to achieve it have changed.

In the past, search engines matched results to simple keywords. You could get results with keyword stuffing and SEO hacks. A lone SEO specialist could move the needle for a brand with basic optimization and content creation.

Today, Google uses many algorithms to serve a single search result. These algorithms don't just read what you type. They understand what you say (in text or out loud); take into account your location and settings; parse hundreds of billions of pages in a search index; use many factors to judge the authority, usability, quality, and relevance of all web pages with possible answers; and serve you the best results. It all happens in a fraction of a second, and Google constantly evolves how these algorithms work. Other search engines follow a similar approach.

Voice further complicates the picture. Instead of all the factors above, a voice search relies on long-tail optimization. Pleasing search engines and consumers with voice requires different content, skills, and strategies.

On top of it all, the stakes have changed. It isn't the year 2000. Search isn't one strategy in an online marketing toolkit. It's the number one way consumers find products and services. If a brand doesn't rank, it doesn't exist. If a brand doesn't appear for relevant queries, it doesn't compete. That means the table stakes for SEO today include the following:

- Conduct keyword research
- Find and prioritize ranking opportunities
- Create content that ranks
- Optimize existing content to rank better
- Conduct technical audits

- Address issues with page speed and usability
- Optimize sites and content for mobile
- Build and execute voice strategies
- Create voice content

These activities require large amounts of labor and resources to do well. Even a well-executed strategy only scratches the surface of what's possible. Search algorithms constantly assess and reassess who and what ranks, which requires constant agility from brands.

Humans alone can't keep up. We lack the bandwidth to evaluate the full spectrum of site and search data required to do effective SEO today. We also can't act on this data consistently fast enough or at scale. At best, we can hire more people to do more work on SEO.

Brands first turned to traditional software to help. SaaS platforms made it easier to find and extract search data. They offered better insight into ranking opportunities and gaps. They also provided basic optimization recommendations based on best practices.

Though helpful, these tools are limited. They still rely on rules hard coded by the same humans who struggle to keep up with SEO activities. They can't adapt if search algorithms suddenly change or new channels become essential. They don't take into account the context around your specific site and search presence. They can't make valuable predictions about search performance beyond offering basic recommendations.

Artificial intelligence for SEO can do all of these things and more.

BERT, MUM, and AI-Powered Search Results

Several AI-powered developments at Google in recent years have big implications on the future of search results and how marketers seek to rank in them. The first we'll look at is BERT.

BERT stands for bidirectional encoder representations from transformers. It's a pretrained language model that Google now applies to search query results and featured snippets. BERT uses NLP, NLU, and sentiment analysis to process every word in a search query in relation to all the other words in a sentence. In the past, Google used to process words one by one in order.

In short, BERT understands the context of searches, not just the keywords in them. It's a big reason marketers are advised to create great content that matches search intent. Keywords are still important, but Google's language models are getting better at interpreting the true intent of a keyword phrase and delivering the content that best matches it.

Another development, MUM, takes this concept even further. Standing for multitask unified model, MUM is "1,000 times more powerful" than BERT, according to Google.[63] MUM understands the full context behind a search and how it relates to your other searches.

Google gives the following example to illustrate MUM's power:

Let's say you ask MUM, "I've hiked Mount Adams and now want to hike Mount Fuji next fall. What should I do differently to prepare?" It's a complex question typically reserved for a human guide. But MUM can understand all the different contexts related to your question. It can actually understand that you're comparing two mountains, you're looking for advice, and preparation can include both gear to buy and a fitness routine. It can then generate a series of responses that address all of these aspects.[64]

MUM is still in its early days, but the power of this technology has massive implications for SEO practitioners. It signals that the future of search may include more than just using AI. It may include creating content that is fuel for a supersmart AI agent layered on top of the world's information.

Use Cases for AI in SEO

Thanks to pattern recognition, AI can identify trends and insights in search data that humans can't. And with NLU, AI can understand the intent behind searches. These capabilities give brands several compelling use cases for AI in SEO.

Conduct Predictive Keyword Research

AI tools for SEO can conduct predictive keyword research at scale. AI recommends search opportunities based on your website's unique authority and content. Brands can see a difficulty score for each search topic customized to their specific domain. They can also rank topics by personalized opportunity scores, making it possible to predict search performance and highlight which opportunities a particular brand should attack and avoid.

Overall, AI tools for SEO eliminate the need for manual keyword research and enable predictions that were impossible to make with traditional software.

Identify Opportunities and Gaps

AI can be used to find opportunities and gaps in search strategy by spotting patterns in the competition's search data. AI tools can evaluate the top pages ranking for a topic, detect how you need to address the topic to compete, show you topic areas the competition failed to address, and predict the search intent behind a topic. For instance, they can tell you if the searcher is looking for information, comparing results, or looking to buy.

Optimize Content for Search

Using NLP, AI optimizes each piece of content you publish and recommends how to make existing content rank higher. It also suggests what topics to cover in new content so it will rank well from the start. It does this by building a smart content brief on a topic that evaluates data from your site, competitors, and search engines. The brief suggests topics you must cover to rank, determines the minimum quality level and word count needed to compete, and recommends links to include and questions to answer. That makes it easier to rack up quick SEO wins. You can evaluate an existing content piece and update it, or you can build a brief for your next article to give it a great shot at success.

Manage Business Listings

Search engines display business listings that include information such as address, contact information, and hours of operation. Since these business listings serve as a critical reference for consumers, an inaccurate listing can harm brand equity and impact sales. But keeping listings accurate is a challenge. Changes to listings don't always update in real time, and it's tough to monitor and navigate all the search engines, maps, apps, and voice assistants where a single listing might appear.

AI-powered SEO platforms help brands manage local and global business listings at scale by making listing additions, removals, and updates easier, and by automatically detecting listing inconsistencies and inaccuracies. The result? Less time spent managing listings and more time spent creating great search experiences for consumers.

Vendors to Explore

It's clear that search engines depend on AI to serve the right results to users, but how do you make sure that your content is the result served? SEO isn't as simple anymore as creating a great article and updating it periodically to stay ranked. As search engines become more complex so they can handle the enormous glut of information being published online every second—and to adjust to the change of how voice assistant searches are conducted—entrepreneurs have found a rich market among SEOs that needs AI to handle modern search.

At Marketing AI Institute, we've used or reviewed a number of AI-powered SEO tools that we believe are worth a look if you're in the market for some machine assistance.

BrightEdge

BrightEdge (www.brightedge.com) uses AI to discover what people are searching for, helping them create a content strategy that captures more traffic. The BrightEdge platform gives SEOs real-time insights into consumer search. It recommends what to do to rank, and forecasts the business impact of search actions. The company's AI can perform such tasks as conduct keyword research and predict traffic gains to identify search intent signals. It's a unified platform that improves SEO performance using the power of machine learning.

HubSpot

HubSpot (www.hubspot.com) has SEO features that use AI to make search optimization easier as part of its marketing automation platform. HubSpot brainstorms what to write so you rank well for topics important to your business. It reads your site content, makes optimization recommendations, and even suggests ways to structure and link your content into a single cohesive pillar and topic cluster strategy. It's a less manual and more intelligent way to do basic SEO tasks. This frees marketers for more important, more creative work.

MarketMuse

MarketMuse (www.marketmuse.com) uses AI to predict and improve search performance. The platform evaluates all content on your domain, then highlights opportunities to improve existing content and rank new articles. It also considers competing content that ranks well, then delivers advice on how to outrank it. A heatmap that identifies competitor strengths and weaknesses is included. MarketMuse even provides a personalized difficulty score that shows you which topics are easier and harder for you to rank based on your domain. You can predict which topics will be most successful, and prioritize your investments before committing time and money to SEO actions.

Yext

Yext (www.yext.com) uses AI to keep business listings and information current across hundreds of platforms, including search engines, local search results, and voice search. It does this by managing a brand's business listings, online reputation, and reviews. It optimizes the brand's web pages to improve its presence in search, and makes sure the data is formatted properly for both search and voice. Yext even provides AI-powered site search that extracts relevant information from unstructured documents on your site, and then serves relevant information to visitors when they search or ask questions. These capabilities wouldn't be possible without the speed, scale, and smarts of AI.

Voice and the Future of Search

AI hasn't just changed how we write content that ranks. It has enabled an entirely new search medium: voice search.

AI makes Alexa, Siri, and other voice assistants possible in the first place. NLP and NLG make sure voice assistants offer accurate, understandable, and helpful responses. As a result, consumers have embraced voice as a valuable, frictionless channel to search and buy. In fact, Juniper Research predicts that voice assistants will drive $80 billion in commerce per year by 2023.[65]

Brands can't afford to ignore the opportunity presented by voice search. But voice requires different strategies and skills, say voice experts Scot and Susan Westwater of Pragmatic Digital.

"A lot of brands understand search and are doing optimization already. The key difference [with voice] is, instead of keywords, you're focusing on long-tail search . . . Do not take your content from the website and slap it into a voice experience."[66]

Instead, brands need to consider the entire customer journey. What problems are you trying to solve for prospects? What do people ask about your product or service? What do they want to learn from you or about your industry? Brands must turn answers to these questions into snippets of natural conversation to power a voice strategy.

Getting this right from the start matters more than you might expect. Voice is often a zero-sum game. Instead of presenting pages of search results for a user to browse, voice serves a single answer. To get noticed, you don't just need to be good; you need to be the best. And you'll need to experiment to figure out what works "because," according to the Westwaters, "voice is relatively new, there aren't established user patterns. If you want to understand how people will interact with your brand on voice, the only way to do it is to create something!"[67]

Chapter 14

Social Media Marketing and AI

If anyone has their pulse on the future of technol-
ogy, it's Gary Vaynerchuk. Vaynerchuk is a giant in the social media and
business worlds, and for good reason. In the late 1990s, Vaynerchuk successfully leveraged the internet to take his family liquor store from $3 mil-
lion to $60 million in sales within five years. He then built VaynerMedia,
a full-service digital agency that uses his proven social media playbook to
grow brands. But Vaynerchuk has the same problem every other social
media marketer has: He can't be everywhere at once.

Consumers use hundreds of social media and content channels.
Vaynerchuk's business depends on capturing attention across all of them.
With more than twelve million combined followers across social media
channels, he's doing pretty well so far. But consumers are ravenous for
fresh content in different formats across different channels, and even the
legendary GaryVee needed a little help. That's why he turned to artificial
intelligence.

Vaynerchuk and team used an AI social media tool called Lately to
supercharge their social content. Lately uses AI to autogenerate social
media posts from podcasts, videos, and text articles. Once you upload

an article, video, or audio file to Lately, it extracts interesting tidbits and turns them into engaging social shares.

The VaynerMedia team used Lately to power GaryVee TV, a Twitter channel the company launched in 2020. GaryVee TV shares the best quotes and clips from Vaynerchuk's daily life as a CEO. Lately autogenerates much of the content, and it produces results. Vaynerchuk saw a *12,000 percent* increase in content engagement from shares that were created using Lately.[68]

Humans are still an essential part of the process. AI automates most of the tedious work required to generate hundreds of social media shares, but human creativity is needed to add the polish and pizzazz that gets the shares over the finish line. It's the perfect example of how humans and machines can work together to do better, more efficient marketing. And it's just the tip of the iceberg when it comes to AI's impact on the world of social media.

AI-Powered Influence and Engagement

Any social media platform you use today, either as a consumer or a marketer, relies heavily on AI to serve content to users, determine what content will keep users on the platform, and suggest additional content to keep them coming back. This makes the job of a social media marketer a difficult one, requiring you to guess, estimate, and hypothesize what social media content will both resonate with human audiences and receive preference from machine algorithms.

The problem is that social media pros are often great at the human side, deploying smart strategies and compelling creatives that capture the attention of individual consumers, but they have little to no data-backed insight into what works for humans and algorithms at scale. Perhaps, paradoxically, the solution to performing well on social media platforms that rely on AI is to use more AI, to fight machines with more machines that offer unique advantages when it comes to performance—and protection—on social media.

Today, AI-powered social media tools abound that can use data to predict which posts will work, create posts automatically, detect consumer trends that humans can't, and moderate comments. As a result, AI is increasingly becoming essential for brands that rely on social media channels as key performance drivers.

Consumer behavior dictates that brands engage with consumers in a personalized, helpful, and authentic way on social media channels, building real communities and relationships around shared interests and topics. Yet most find it difficult to break through the noise; drive real marketing results from social media that matter to executives; and protect themselves in a chaotic world of charged conversations, where expensive, brand-ruining backlash can occur from a single post. That might be why AI for the social media market is projected to grow from $633 million in 2018 to more than $2.1 billion by 2023.[69]

AI-powered technology is starting to add massive value to social media marketers overwhelmed by data, tasks, and dangers related to social media. It does that by helping social media professionals process a firehose of data on individual behaviors, preferences, beliefs, interests, physical habits, and travel. It makes sense of what individuals write, post, and comment on, which groups individuals engage with, and which brands individuals review. Smart social media marketers use AI to automate tedious tasks, scale up their strategies, and produce data-driven campaigns that actually get results.

Use Cases for AI in Social Media

Because of its business value, AI is being used today across a number of use cases to make social media more effective and efficient.

Predict Visual and Creative Performance

Thanks to developments in computer vision and image recognition, AI can detect which individual visual elements are creating engagement from users on social media, then make recommendations about how to create better visual social content based on this information. It can predict which colors, fonts, visuals, and image formatting should be mixed and matched in any given social post to drive maximum shares, comments, and, most importantly, clicks across content. This gives social media community managers a data-backed way to make intelligent recommendations on visual content and produce creatives that are proven to deliver better results.

Create Social Media Content Automatically at Scale

AI can create social media content for you by using NLP and NLG to analyze and generate human-sounding language. By processing your existing content (blogs, audio, video), AI can extract the most compelling snippets based on historical data and turn those into engaging social media posts. With just a few clicks, social media marketers can then distribute these posts across channels, while AI tools monitor and learn from performance. It's a way to do what social media professionals do best, but it's faster and better. Humans determine messaging and direction of social campaigns, while machines handle the heavy lifting of producing hundreds of social shares.

Detect Social Trends and Consumer Insights

User-generated content on social media networks is used by AI tools to detect consumer patterns that help brands understand consumers better and tailor social campaigns to preferences. AI tools do this by analyzing the content and tone of text comments and by profiling individual consumers based on visuals in their posts that indicate demographics, brand loyalty, and dozens of other characteristics. AI tools then surface these insights to arm brands with large amounts of data to inform how they market to audiences across social platforms and in other digital campaigns.

This is a level of real-time insight that human analysts working on their own just can't match, and it's providing brands with new, valuable ways to win markets and moments minute-by-minute on social channels.

Moderate Comments

By analyzing content, tone, and sentiment, AI is used today to moderate comments across social media networks, both by the networks themselves and by brands looking to protect their brand equity and audiences across channels.

AI-powered tools use the language processing capabilities described in other use cases above to detect dangerous or problematic social media comments and take action to moderate them by automatically removing them. Because of AI's ability to do this at scale, it can keep up with floods of inappropriate, illegal, or spam comments in real time. This is a job that is both impossible and inadvisable for community managers to do on their own. AI makes their jobs more effective and keeps managers happier by doing the dirtiest work for them.

Vendors to Explore

Social media platforms are a critical piece of any digital marketing program, but it's hard to use them in a cost-effective way. That's why entrepreneurs are eagerly developing AI solutions to help social media marketers do more. This has resulted in plenty of dynamic companies with AI-powered social media solutions that use data to determine what drives engagement and results on social media channels.

Here is a collection of AI vendors in the social media space that we've reviewed, profiled, or used that you may find worthy of further exploration.

Buffer

Buffer (www.buffer.com) offers a number of social media publishing tools that automate some of the legwork that goes into building an audience online. Buffer's engagement features leverage machine learning and sentiment analysis to help you prioritize conversations. It also delivers smart alerts that surface posts with questions or negative comments so you can address those first.

Lately

Lately (www.lately.ai) uses AI to automatically turn blogs, videos, and podcasts into dozens of high-performing social media posts. The solution does this by assessing your existing content and using that information to create engaging snippets of text, audio, and video for social media—all adapted to fit your voice and brand. Lately can even use competitor social media data to train on, so you can get a leg up on your competition. As a result, brands using Lately are able to create more content in less time while connecting with customers faster. This generates more engagement, leads, and revenue from social media marketing.

Linkfluence

Linkfluence (www.linkfluence.com) helps companies detect consumer trends across social media channels with the help of AI-powered analysis. It uses machine learning and NLP to collect, structure, and analyze data from hundreds of millions of social media posts, then surfaces insights brands can use to drive business and marketing decisions. The solution also uses computer vision technology to identify logos, emotions, and demographics in social posts to help brands understand how consumers engage with products and services.

Unlike traditional surveys, focus groups, and interviews, Linkfluence's AI-powered social media intelligence delivers less bias and more statistical reliability to brands in real time.

Smart Moderation

Smart Moderation (www.smartmoderation.com) uses AI to automatically moderate comments across social media platforms and websites. The solution's AI analyzes language in comments across channels and identifies those that are inappropriate, spammy, or even illegal. It then takes action to erase problematic comments in real time. This takes a huge burden off community managers and makes sure brands are protected from damaging engagements online, allowing social media marketers to get back to building compelling campaigns that drive quality engagement.

Sprout Social

Sprout Social (www.sproutsocial.com) is a social media platform that leverages AI and machine learning to create more intelligent automation online. As part of its Twitter automation features, Sprout Social uses machine learning to suggest replies to incoming Twitter messages. It reads a tweet, then suggests a response you can post with a couple of clicks. It's a smarter way to create more engagement in less time on social media.

Manipulation and Misinformation in the Machine Age

Unfortunately, the use of AI in social media also has a dark side. Social media companies rely on network effects to build massive businesses and win market share. The more people who use a platform, the more valuable and influential the platform becomes. As a result, every social media giant relies on AI to serve content users find engaging. Algorithms determine what you see, and they're optimized for maximum engagement, which isn't always a good thing.

The 2016 US presidential election wasn't the first time these algorithms were abused, but it was a game-changing example of how to abuse AI. Cambridge Analytica, a consultancy for Donald Trump's campaign, used data from tens of millions of Facebook users to game the platform's algorithms. The organization engineered shares that promoted fake news and incendiary content to influence voters by manipulating emotions. As more users engaged with these posts, Facebook's algorithms rewarded Cambridge Analytica with more reach.

Cambridge Analytica was just the beginning. During COVID-19, Facebook became a major source of misinformation about vaccinations. The platform's algorithms rewarded content that offended or outraged. At times, it seemed Facebook directly profited off the increased engagement created by lies, hate speech, and misinformation. As a result, the company was perceived as slow—or even unwilling—to act. Whether this was intentional is unclear. What is clear is that the problem isn't going away soon. CEO Mark Zuckerberg has said AI is the only way to effectively police content. "Translation: The problem is so big that humans alone can't police the service," writes Jeremy Kahn in *Fortune*,[70] reporting on Facebook's AI.

Facebook isn't alone. YouTube's algorithms commonly recommend conspiracy theory videos. Twitter has been cited time and time again for inadequately policing hate speech on its platform. Social media companies lack the will or the technology to regulate manipulation, hate speech, and lies on their platforms. This presents a dilemma, and a duty, for marketers.

Brands may be tempted to use manipulative messaging and incendiary content to capture attention. They may even be temporarily rewarded for it by social media algorithms. But in the long term, such behaviors damage brand equity and harm society. Done often enough, they destroy consumer trust and negatively impact mental and physical health.

Every brand claims to have values. Values-first brands are proven to win in the marketplace. But actually following through on those values is another matter. When algorithms reward us for manipulation, marketers must take responsibility for their actions and strategies.

The real test of brand values comes from choosing to market ethically, even when you're rewarded in the short term for doing the opposite. We do that by committing to the creation of real value and real connections with consumers. We do it by rejecting algorithmic hacks and manipulative messaging. To use social media technology responsibly, we actually must commit to being humans first, marketers second.

Chapter 15

Scaling AI

In April 2018, McKinsey Global Institute published a discussion paper based on an analysis of more than four hundred AI use cases across nineteen industries and nine business functions. The goal of the paper was to highlight the broad use and economic potential of advanced AI techniques.[71]

The research found that AI, including all the forms of machine learning and deep learning evaluated, had the potential to create $9.5–$15.4 trillion in annual value for the global economy. For context, the United States' gross domestic product, or the total value of all final goods and services produced in a country, in 2018 was $20.6 trillion.

Across business functions, McKinsey Global Institute projected impact on HR, finance and IT, product development, service operations, strategy and corporate finance, risk, supply chain management and manufacturing, other operations, and marketing and sales. Of the nine areas, it was marketing and sales that led the way with a forecast of $3.3–$6.0 trillion in annual value created by AI. This value was based on forecasts within seven marketing- and sales-related business problems:

1. Pricing and promotion ($0.9–$1.9 trillion)
2. Customer service management ($497.6 billion–$1.0 trillion)

3. Next product to buy / individualized offering ($0.7–$1.0 trillion)
4. Customer acquisition / lead generation ($361.5 billion–$0.7 trillion)
5. Marketing budget allocation ($410.3 billion–$0.6 trillion)
6. Churn ($205.9–$379.1 billion)
7. Channel management ($218.2–$319.6 billion)

While the impact varies by industry, each of these areas offers a reference point to help you begin to consider the tangible financial impact AI can have on your business. Industries in which digital interactions with consumers are frequent will see the greatest potential for returns from AI. These regular interactions through websites, emails, mobile apps, voice assistants, and Internet of Things devices create large data sets based on behavior and intent signals that can be used to continually train and improve AI applications. The report specifically calls out consumer packaged goods, banking, telecommunications, high tech, travel, insurance, media and entertainment, and retail.

Using McKinsey Global Institute's interactive data visualization tool[72] that was released with the research, you can drill into specific industries to gain a deeper understanding of AI's potential impact. For example, in retail, which is projected to realize $1.1 trillion in value creation within marketing and sales, more than half comes from value that is unlocked in the pricing and promotion category.

According to the discussion paper, "In retail, marketing and sales is the area with the most significant potential value from AI, and within that function, pricing and promotion and customer service management are the main value areas. Our use cases show that using customer data to personalize promotions, for example, including tailoring individual offers every day, can lead to a 1 to 2 percent increase in incremental sales for brick-and-mortar retailers alone."

AI + Creativity

One interesting omission from the McKinsey Global Institute model is the potential financial impact of AI on creativity. As we have seen in earlier chapters, AI already is capable of playing a major supporting role in the creative process, including video and music production, branding, art and graphic design, copywriting, editing, and problem solving. And some would argue that AI does not stop at just assisting humans, but actually possesses the potential to be creative itself. So is AI creative? There are three sides to this debate:

1. AI will become an increasingly powerful tool to enhance human creativity, but it cannot be creative on its own.
2. AI has the potential to be creative, but current technology is not there yet.
3. AI can be creative now.

In order to determine the truth, we first need to agree on what creativity is. But therein lies the problem.

According to Merriam-Webster, *creativity* is simply defined as "the ability to create." And *create* means "to bring into existence." So under these broad definitions, it's logical to say that yes, a machine can be creative if it generates something tangible such as a literary work or piece of art.

Meanwhile, the *Oxford Advanced Learner's Dictionary* defines *creativity* as "the use of skill and imagination to produce something new or to produce art." *Imagination* is the keyword here because it implies the ability to form an image or concept in your mind of something new. Yes, a machine can create art and language and solve complex problems in unique ways, but is it actually imagining anything, or is it just using its training data and math to create an output?

This debate over machine creativity was brought to life in game two of the AlphaGo versus Go world champion Lee Sedol match in 2016 that we described in chapter one. Move 37, as it became known, saw the DeepMind machine place a stone on the Go board in a nontraditional spot that had human Go experts baffled. Michael Redmond, a commentator on the live English broadcast and a top Go player himself, said at the time, "I wasn't expecting that. I don't really know if it's a good or bad move. It's a very strange move."

Sedol, who had already lost game one to the machine, was in disbelief. He stared at the board for a moment, sat back in his chair, and spent the next twelve minutes assessing his options before finally making his next move. Sedol never recovered. He would lose game two, and AlphaGo would go on to win the best-of-five series, four to one.

The DeepMind team had trained AlphaGo using deep learning, specifically a type called reinforcement learning in which AlphaGo learned to discover new strategies by playing millions of Go games against versions of itself. In addition, AlphaGo learned the ancient game by studying millions of moves made by top human Go players.

Cade Metz, an author and technology correspondent with the *New York Times*, was in Seoul, South Korea, covering the match for *Wired* magazine. He spoke with DeepMind's David Silver, the lead researcher on the AlphaGo project, about Move 37. Metz summarized what happened in this way:

"So AlphaGo learns from human moves, and then it learns from moves made when it plays itself. It understands how humans play, but it can also look beyond how humans play to an entirely different level of the game. This is what happened with Move 37 . . . AlphaGo had calculated that there was a one-in-ten-thousand chance that a human would make that move. But when it drew on all the knowledge it had accumulated by playing itself so many times—and looked ahead to the future of the game—it decided to make the move anyway. And the move was genius."[73]

In *AlphaGo–The Movie*, Silver said of Move 37 that AlphaGo "went beyond its human guide, and it came up with something new, and creative, and different."[74] But in the documentary, Silver also made the point that this is not human versus machine, but rather human plus machine. "AlphaGo is human-created, and I think that's the ultimate sign of human ingenuity and cleverness. Everything that AlphaGo does, it does because a human has either created the data that it learns from, created the learning algorithm that learns from that data, or created the search algorithm.

All of these things have come from humans. So, really, this is a human endeavor."[75]

Sedol would later say, "I thought AlphaGo was based on probability calculation and that it was merely a machine. But when I saw this move, I changed my mind. Surely, AlphaGo is creative. This move was really creative and beautiful."[76]

Debating the question of whether AI can be truly creative is a fun thought experiment, but no matter which side you come down on, the future impact of AI on creativity is indisputable.

My take is that machines are creators; they just are not creative in the traditional human sense. Yes, a machine can write a song or even a play or a book, once it has been trained on the writing style, but human creativity comes from the sum of our experiences, knowledge, senses, emotions, and capabilities. A machine does not feel anything when it writes lyrics. It does not draw on its emotions to inspire its words or actions. A machine calculates probabilities and produces outputs based on data.

But at the end of the day, all that matters to you and your business is that AI will accelerate your ability to create and personalize content and experiences at scale. Machines can create, and they can inspire human creativity. The value that can be unlocked as a result is immense.

A Blueprint to Scaling AI

As the McKinsey Global Institute paper highlights, the financial reward for successfully scaling AI is significant, but the reality is that most businesses are still in the infancy of AI adoption. According to our "2021 State of Marketing AI Report" research, while 52 percent of marketers say AI is very or critically important to the success of their marketing in the next twelve months, only 17 percent said they were in the scaling phase of marketing AI transformation, which is characterized by wide-scale adoption of AI that is consistently producing efficiency and performance results.[77]

But don't let the slow adoption and lack of economic impact to date fool you into thinking AI's effect on you and your business will be limited. The learning curve and costs associated with deploying AI technology serve as barriers to entry for many leaders and businesses. As these subside and the technology becomes more prevalent and easier to apply, AI's contribution to growth and value within enterprises will rapidly accelerate.

The early movers who figure out how to adapt their organizations and infuse smarter technology into every aspect of their business and marketing will build nearly insurmountable competitive advantages. But the window of opportunity to seize an early mover advantage is short. You have to act now to put AI at the foundation of your marketing talent, technology, and strategy. Here are ten steps to help you scale AI in your company:

1. Think Strategically

It's easy to get overwhelmed by AI if you do not understand it. At its most basic level, AI is just smarter marketing technology, so think about it the same way you would every other marketing technology investment.

AI needs to solve real business problems by reducing costs or increasing revenue. There is no magic AI button that makes your marketing and business more intelligent. You cannot buy just a single AI platform to replace all your existing technologies. AI is built to perform narrow, specific tasks at superhuman levels. Your marketing technology stack will likely expand, which obviously creates complexity if you do not plan ahead. Success with AI requires an understanding of what it is and what it is capable of doing (and not doing), as well as experimentation, patience, and a strategic vision.

2. View Data as Essential to AI Success

A great starting point for thinking about the potential value of AI is to assess opportunities to get more out of your data. For example, if your marketing team spends significant time organizing and visualizing performance analytics and developing narratives to tell the story of what is happening and why, that can all be intelligently automated. You can also look across your marketing and consider all the ways you use data, or should be using data, to make predictions and improve customer experiences.

According to Accenture, "Having a data strategy to underpin your AI strategy is critical for competitive advantage and will ultimately help accelerate your time to value. In fact, 72 percent of Strategic Scalers (those who are successfully scaling AI in their organizations) said a core data foundation has been key to their success."[78]

As part of your data strategy, you will need to consider how data is acquired, cleansed, labeled, and structured; where it is stored; and in what ways it can be used to make your marketing more intelligent. Your data strategy also must take into account security, bias, and privacy concerns, especially when related to personally identifiable information and highly regulated industries.

3. Become an Informed Buyer of AI-Powered Technology

As we highlighted in chapter three, marketers who lack confidence in evaluating AI-powered marketing technology will struggle to identify smarter solutions that can drive efficiency and performance. As your understanding of AI technology grows, you will have a greater chance of finding the right technologies and creating value for your company.

Use the Marketer-to-Machine Scale as a starting point when evaluating your existing marketing technologies and researching new AI-powered solutions to add to your tech stack.

4. Prioritize Use Cases to Pilot

The most effective way to approach marketing AI in the early stages of adoption is to focus on one use case at a time, since AI is built to do specific tasks (e.g., optimize email send time, predict lead conversions, write email subject lines, recommend content to users).

One of the foremost thought leaders on AI today is Andrew Ng. He is the founder of DeepLearning.AI, general partner at AI Fund, chairman and cofounder of Coursera, an adjunct professor at Stanford University, and formerly the chief scientist at Baidu and the founding lead of the Google Brain team. In his "AI Transformation Playbook," Ng states, "It is more important for your first few AI projects to succeed rather than be the most valuable AI projects. They should be meaningful enough so that the initial successes will help your company gain familiarity with AI and also convince others in the company to invest in further AI projects; they should not be so small that others would consider it trivial. The important thing is to get the flywheel spinning so that your AI team can gain momentum."[79]

So in the early going, think about stacking a series of successful pilot projects as a way to build a strong foundation for your marketing AI transformation.

5. Define Priority Business Goals and Challenges

The two primary business outcomes of AI initiatives will be reducing costs and accelerating revenue. For many organizations just starting with marketing AI, cost-saving use cases and projects are likely to be the most logical for gaining early wins and executive support. However, as you begin to scale, you will want to develop a near-term vision for how to use AI to grow revenue through language, vision, and prediction applications that improve customer experience and help identify new markets and opportunities. Here are some common AI-powered business outcomes to consider and prioritize for your business:

- Accelerating revenue growth
- Creating personalized consumer experiences at scale
- Driving costs down
- Generating greater ROI on campaigns
- Getting more actionable insights from marketing data
- Improving customer retention
- Increasing lead volume and quality
- Optimizing pricing and promotions

- Predicting consumer needs and behaviors with greater accuracy
- Reducing time spent on repetitive, data-driven tasks
- Removing friction from customer service
- Shortening the sales cycle
- Unlocking greater value from marketing technologies

6. Educate and Engage Leadership

As we touched on in chapter four, there is a reasonable probability that some of your early pilot projects won't meet the goals your team sets. But you can't let early setbacks stall your long-term plans to build a smarter business.

You are going to need the leadership team involved in the process. They must understand the potential short-term challenges, embrace the value of learning through experimentation, and provide the resources necessary to evolve your talent, technology, and strategies. Be clear in your plans, communicate with consistency and clarity, and always connect your AI initiatives with business goals and metrics that matter to company leaders.

7. Reimagine Your Marketing Team

Your marketing team five years from now may look nothing like it does today. Roles such as marketing AI specialist, AI ops leader, AI trainer, machine manager, recommendation engine director, director of deep learning, VP of augmented intelligence, and chief algorithms officer could all find their way into your organizational structure and redefine the knowledge and skills needed to drive your growth.

At Stitch Fix, an online personal styling company with a market cap of more than $2 billion, astrophysicists have traded careers researching the universe and simulating galaxies on supercomputers to build recommendation engines that predict customers' personal tastes and styles.

In a *Wired* magazine article, author Arielle Pardes wrote, "Stitch Fix doesn't ask its clients to self-identify with labels like 'preppy' or 'boho.'

Instead, it collects data on what people like through their purchases and through tools like Style Shuffle, a Tinder-for-clothes where people can 'like' or 'dislike' specific items. In the aggregate, that data makes up Style Space—a map of all the things clients 'like' and the way they relate to each other."[80]

Stitch Fix uses these models to predict what else customers will like, similar to how Netflix recommends shows and Spotify learns your musical tastes.

Your company may not be hiring astrophysicists any time soon, but it's important to realize that disruption is coming from places you may not expect. Every business in every industry is susceptible to being made obsolete by someone who uses AI to build a smarter business model. Start taking the steps needed now to move your business forward by reimaging roles and career paths and identifying AI-driven marketing agencies and consulting firms that can help you level up your capabilities as you invest in upskilling your team.

Become an Algorithmic Leader

In *The Algorithmic Leader: How to Be Smart When the Machines Are Smarter Than You*, author and futurist Mike Walsh defines an algorithmic leader as someone who has successfully adapted their decision-making, management style, and creative output to the complexities of the machine age. Walsh explains that algorithmic leaders embrace new ideas that could never have become a reality before the age of artificial intelligence. They do not simply look at intelligent algorithms as tools but rather as an evolved way to approach and solve problems. They see AI as a vehicle to move away from incremental improvements in pursuit of exponential growth and true digital transformation.

"If you are simply automating your existing processes, adding a chatbot to your website, or updating your mobile app, then in all probability you are not thinking big enough about your future opportunities. Too often, digital transformation is just digital incrementalism," says Walsh. "Part of the journey to becoming an algorithmic leader is being brave enough to pursue opportunities that deliver results in multiples, not just margins."[81]

8. Train Your Team and Explore AI Together

Our "2021 State of Marketing AI Report" shows that 70 percent of marketers say a lack of education and training is the top barrier to AI adoption. In addition, 82 percent of businesses do not have internal AI-focused education and training. This has to change for the industry and your business to achieve what is possible with AI.[82]

As we have learned throughout this book, AI will be integrated into every aspect of marketing and will impact the roles and responsibilities of every professional. If you are going to unlock the value AI can create, you are going to need learning programs that are designed to engage and advance your entire marketing team.

Tassilo Festetics, VP of global solutions at Anheuser-Busch InBev, took his entire team for a weeklong immersive experience in AI and said, "It is important for the team to understand the basics of machine learning and AI to be able to identify game-changing opportunities for the company, be it commercial, supply, logistics, or employee-related topics."[83]

At PR 20/20, we created an AI readiness training program that features three-month professional development intensives dedicated to the understanding and adoption of AI across the team. Each quarter includes the following:

- Core topic (e.g., definition of AI, AI and business fundamentals, how to buy smarter tech, and AI ethics)
- Book club
- Professional development sessions with presentations and Q&A
- Recommended weekly reading

- Featured talks and courses
- Certifications

This approach also inspired our Marketing Al Institute Al Academy for Marketers online education platform (www.marketingacademy.ai), which features on-demand courses, certifications, learning paths, and resources to help marketers pilot and scale Al in their companies.

Al education in the enterprise needs to be a constantly evolving initiative as the technology advances at such a rapid pace. The knowledge and skills your team needs will be a moving target, and marketers must constantly upgrade themselves to stay ahead of the curve and remain relevant.

Lessons Learned in Higher Education

While we all face the challenges of keeping up with Al technology and how it affects our talent and strategies, the difficulties are magnified in higher education, where school leaders battle every day to prepare students for the future. They must figure out how to adapt curriculum and experiences, how to find professors who can teach the latest innovations, and how to predict which career paths will become extinct and which new ones will emerge. They also need to remain competitive with the rapidly growing availability of online courses and professional certifications from technology companies like Google and Microsoft. All this has to be done while addressing budget constraints, governmental rules and regulations, and a shrinking population.

In *Robot-Proof: Higher Education in the Age of Artificial Intelligence*, Joseph E. Aoun, president of Northeastern University, states that regardless of industry or profession, graduates will need the following:

- Data literacy to read, analyze, and use information

- Human literacy to understand humanities, communication, and design
- Technological literacy for a grounding in coding and engineering principles[84]

So, what are universities doing to adapt?

According to the *Chronicle for Higher Education*, the University of Florida may be creating a blueprint for others to follow with its $125 million project to power a new AI academic program across all disciplines. The initiative began with provost Joseph Glover's desire for a nonsiloed data-science program and was catalyzed by a $25 million donation from Chris Malachowsky, a Florida alum and cofounder of NVIDIA. Inventor of the graphics processing unit (GPU), which revolutionized the gaming industry and powered the deep-learning revolution, NVIDIA offered another $25 million in in-kind donations, and tens of millions of dollars more would come in from private donors and the state of Florida. The result was one of the most powerful supercomputers on any American campus, opening up new possibilities to advance research, introduce certificates and degrees centered on AI competency, and educate students across every subject area and major.

"We believe that AI shouldn't be limited to the computer science department or to one institution," says Glover. "Making sure that students across the curriculum learn about AI gives us the opportunity to train people at scale for tomorrow's jobs."[85]

NVIDIA leaders believe the University of Florida's program can serve as a model for other higher education institutions to prepare students for an AI-powered future.

"What we see now at Florida is absolutely replicable," says Cheryl Martin, director of higher education and research at NVIDIA. "We're putting together ways to package the Florida model so other universities can also take on AI."[86]

"UF can be the pioneer for this," says Austin Carson, senior manager of government relations at NVIDIA. "The comprehensive nature of Florida's program sets a strong example for universities across the country. It covers the entire state, is designed to be inclusive, invests in more AI talent and includes across-the-campus curriculum."[87]

9. Focus on Mutual Learning Between Humans and Machines

According to a major 2020 study from MIT Sloan Management Review, BCG GAMMA, and BCG Henderson Institute, only 10 percent of organizations are achieving significant financial benefits with AI.[88]

The research team surveyed three thousand managers and interviewed executives and scholars. They found that more than half of all respondents' companies were piloting or deploying AI (57 percent), have an AI strategy (59 percent), and understand how AI can generate business value (70 percent), which were all significant increases over their survey four years earlier. Yet despite this increased investment and optimism, only one in ten were realizing significant benefits.

So what are the leading organizations doing to outpace their peers? They are focused on continuous organizational learning, the process of creating, retaining, and transferring knowledge within an organization, specifically between humans and machines.

"Isolated AI applications can be powerful. But we find that organizations leading with AI haven't changed processes to use AI. Instead, they've learned with AI how to change processes. The key isn't teaching the machines. Or even learning from the machines. The key is learning with the machines—systematically and continuously," says report coauthor Sam Ransbotham, professor of Information Systems at the Boston College Carroll School of Management.

According to the report, organizations that learn with AI share three essential characteristics:

1. They facilitate systematic and continuous learning between humans and machines.
2. They develop multiple ways for humans and machines to interact.
3. They change to learn, and learn to change.

The model organizations that systematically invest in these activities are 73 percent more likely to achieve significant impact with AI.

"The single most critical driver of value from AI is not algorithms, nor technology—it is the human in the equation," says report coauthor Shervin Khodabandeh, senior partner and managing director at BCG. "We continue to see that despite more companies investing in AI technologies and launching AI initiatives, only a small fraction get meaningful value. What this select group does well is that they create integrated AI-Human systems, where AI learns from humans and humans learn from AI. And the more different ways of learning between the two, the more value there is to get."

10. Consider How AI Can Make Your Brand More Human

In the process of making marketing more intelligent, AI has the potential to make brands more human by enabling marketers to focus increased time and energy on listening, relationship building, creativity, empathy, culture, and community. AI should make us better people, professionals, and brands. However, this will not happen without a focus on privacy, ethics, and morals. AI can be used for good or for evil. You have the choice.

Think about how the rudimentary marketing technology we have access to today is already used to manipulate opinions, emotions, and behaviors. Now imagine that technology is ten times, or even one hundred times, more powerful.

AI constantly learns and never forgets. It can be trained to leverage individual behaviors, preferences, fears, beliefs, and interests to personalize experiences. It knows where you have been, where you are going, who you are with, what you have written in your emails, what you have asked of your voice assistants, what songs you listen to, what mood you are in, what groups you belong to, what stores you shop at, and more. And it can use all of this information to provide the right product at the right time, sometimes before you even know you need it.

Next-gen marketers consider the ramifications of the AI technology they create and use. We truly believe AI will have a disproportionate net positive impact on the industry and society, but it will alter career paths, displace jobs, and continually chip away at our privacy as consumers. We have to be willing to have the hard conversations as an industry now, to make sure we do not ruin what will be the most transformative technological shift we experience in our lifetimes.

We dive deeper into what it takes to build human-centered AI and become more human as a brand in the next chapter.

Chapter 16

More Human

Even the best brands in the world struggle to get AI right. In late 2019, entrepreneur David Heinemeier Hansson shared a story online about his new Apple Card. Apple Card is a credit card product from the maker of the iPhone. It's beautiful, simple, and useful, just like other Apple products. But it had a problem at launch. It was a misogynist.

Hansson and his wife both applied for the card. Both are entrepreneurs with similar incomes. Yet the algorithm behind the card gave Hansson a whopping twenty times more available credit than his wife. He took to Twitter, where his story went viral, prompting a response from Apple.

What happened next has major implications for business and marketing leaders. Apple representatives were respectful of his concern that the card's algorithm was sexist. But they said it was the algorithm's fault. Nobody seemed to know how the algorithm worked, or how to fix it. That's because Apple didn't create the algorithm. They had outsourced its development to Goldman Sachs.

While Apple scrambled, Hansson published a tweetstorm that torched the brand online while the entire world watched. The issue went so viral that Apple's legendary cofounder Steve Wozniak chimed in. It turns out the same thing happened to *his* wife. Wozniak even said Apple bore responsibility for the incident.

As Hansson put it on Twitter, "Apple has handed the customer experience and their reputation as an inclusive organization over to a biased, sexist algorithm it does not understand, cannot reason with, and is unable to control."[89]

It was a brutal episode for a beloved brand. The lesson for business and marketing leaders? If it can happen to a trillion-dollar brand like Apple, it can happen to your brand and business. And it will, unless you take a more human approach to AI starting today.

Bias in AI

Any time you have a race to lead the advancement of a technology like AI, there are people and companies who push forward and challenge what is accepted as normal and ethical. If they don't, then someone else, maybe their competitor, will. Or so the thinking goes.

As consumers, we become desensitized to all the data we're giving up. We willfully share deep insights into our preferences, biases, purchases, locations, friends, and much more. In return, we get personalization. This value exchange between consumers (data) and tech companies (personalization) is what powers many of the AI innovations that are changing our lives.

There are two areas we as marketers and business leaders need to address if we want to use AI responsibly: bias and ethics.

AI is only as good as the data used to train it. There are plenty of ways this data can give AI intentional or unintentional bias. As Apple's mistake shows, bias can be straightforward—it can directly discriminate against a group. Humans inject their own biases, consciously or unconsciously, into data used by AI. Biases can include direct or indirect discrimination based on age, gender, sexual orientation, race, or other characteristics. And this type of bias can do massive harm to brands and individuals. Bias can also simply mean your AI system accidentally produces an unexpected, undesirable output. If your training data is faulty, it may produce bad outcomes.

For instance, if an AI's training data is overexposed to a homogenous market with similar characteristics, its predictions could ignore other, possibly important, market segments, since AI only knows what it's been trained on. Or your AI system could have been trained on data from customers outside a highly regulated industry. This gets certain brands into trouble very fast. An AI system used in the financial services industry but trained outside of it may start targeting prospects by using demographic information, which may end up being illegal.

The lesson is that bias doesn't always have to be directly from a human to be problematic. So how do you address it?

Once you've built or bought a product or system, it's usually too late. You need to address bias at every step of the process that leads to the adoption of AI in products and operations. That includes being able to explain why a system does what it does and how it arrives at conclusions. It also means having visibility into the data the system uses, having some confidence that bias has been minimized, and having steps in place to figure out if the system is exhibiting bias when it goes live.

This isn't easy, even for the best brands and builders. The case of Apple proves this. The company is adept at AI. It has world-class AI researchers and engineering talent. Yet bias still caught it by surprise. When the company discovered the bias, it was too late to do anything about it.

The technology was sound, but the bias considerations were not. That's because fixing bias in AI isn't just a technology problem. Sure, you need to be completely confident your data is comprehensive, accurate, and clean. You also need to have people and processes in place across every business function, not just engineering, to assess bias risks. It's a comprehensive effort, and it takes time to build and use AI for good.

AI for Good

An excellent way to start building and using AI for good is to draft an AI ethics policy for your organization. An AI ethics statement is a formal document that outlines your company's position on AI. It provides specifics on how your company will and won't use AI, and it details what steps you've taken or will take to make sure ethical issues and bias don't affect the AI you build or use.

It's not enough to just publish your policy on your website. People at your organization need to know it exists. They also need to understand why it's important, and they need to believe it carries weight and can be enforced. After all, your teams are the ones who need to consider AI ethics when no one is looking.

The best AI-first companies are not afraid to publicly communicate their commitment to ethics. For example, Adobe has a robust set of ethics, principles, and processes that ensure it's developing responsible AI. The company has committed to broad principles that influence how it builds products, launched an AI ethics committee and review board to help guide product teams, and even uses an AI impact assessment tool during product development to avoid biases.

In Adobe's Commitment to AI Ethics, the company states, "We are committed to ensuring that our technology and the use of our technology benefits society. At Adobe, as we innovate and harness the power of AI in our tools, we are dedicated to addressing the harms posed by biased data in the training of our AI. AI Ethics is one of the core pillars of our commitment to Digital Citizenship, a pledge from Adobe to address the consequences of innovation as part of our role in society."[90]

You can see this commitment in action with Adobe's Neural Filters feature in Photoshop. This AI-powered functionality allows users to add filters, like different types of hair or faces, to images. When Neural Filters was in development, a review board member saw that the tool was problematically displaying a hairstyle of a certain ethnicity. The issue was flagged, and the tool was updated before release. Adobe's AI ethics processes had prevented bias and potential harm to both users and the brand.[91] These kinds of principles and processes are essential for any brand that wants to build or use AI in a responsible manner.

Google also has been recognized for its proactive approach to ethical AI. The company has seven principles that guide its objectives for AI applications.[92] Google believes that AI should:

1. Be socially beneficial
2. Avoid creating or reinforcing unfair bias
3. Be built and tested for safety

4. Be accountable to people
5. Incorporate privacy design principles
6. Uphold high standards of scientific excellence
7. Be made available for uses that accord with these principles

Google has also publicly committed to avoid certain applications of AI. These include:

- Technologies that can cause harm
- Weapons
- Technologies that violate international surveillance norms
- Technologies that contravene international law and human rights

But having a strong code of ethics related to AI and consistently living by that code can be challenging for brands. In December 2020, Google created waves in the industry when it fired Timnit Gebru, its ethical AI colead, after she refused to retract a research paper that examined issues with large language models (LLM), a form of AI technology that is critical to Google's products and innovation. A few months later, following widespread dissent from Google employees and backlash from the scientific community, the company fired Margaret Mitchell, Gebru's coauthor and colead.

Not only are LLMs known to have a high environmental cost due to the processing power they require, but as Karen Hao of *MIT Technology Review* stated in an article about the dangers of language AI, "studies have already shown how racist, sexist, and abusive ideas are embedded in these models. They associate categories like doctors with men and nurses with women, good words with white people and bad ones with Black people. Probe them with the right prompts, and they also begin to encourage things like genocide, self-harm, and child sexual abuse. Because of their size, they have a shockingly high carbon footprint. Because of their fluency, they easily confuse people into thinking a human wrote their outputs, which experts warn could enable the mass production of misinformation."[93]

This demonstrates how challenging the future of AI will be: it's not just about developing principles and processes. We all have individual responsibilities as marketers, too. We will have to make judgment calls about where the ethical lines are as we scale the use of AI.

With AI, we can learn more about consumers than ever before. We can discover their beliefs, interests, fears, and desires. We can use that information to manipulate them. We can make predictions about their behavior and then trigger those behaviors in ways that are unethical. We must focus on using these superpowers for good. But there are, and will continue to be, bad actors. Organizations can use AI to take shortcuts, to put profits over people, to weaponize data, and to conduct psychological warfare through misinformation.

The Dark Side of Artificial Intelligence in Marketing

I spend an inordinate amount of time thinking about AI and its applications for marketing. When writing and speaking about it, I tend to focus on the positive aspects and outcomes.

For businesses, AI can increase efficiency by intelligently automating repetitive tasks, and it can drive revenue by improving an organization's ability to make predictions. For consumers, AI means personalization and convenience: ads that seem to be targeted to your exact interests on every social media channel, voice searches that give you answers on the go, content that solves your problems from brands that seemingly anticipate your needs, and emails with links to products that appear to have been designed just for you. But there's a potential dark side to the technology that makes this all possible. AI is powered by data. The more personal and expansive that data is, the more accurate the predictions become.

Major technology companies are racing to capture as much information about consumers as possible through their interactions online and offline. And the more devices and apps that are enabled to collect their data, the more these companies can learn about their activities, interests, wants, needs, and desires.

Think about the data collection empires these companies are building and all the ways they use technology to learn about us. They know where we are, what we say in emails and text messages, what we buy, who we're with, when we're home, what we eat, how healthy we are, what we read, what we watch, what we listen to, what we search . . . The list could go on for pages.

As marketers, we have the ability to leverage this sort of data to achieve our goals. But the question becomes where to draw the line. What data will your organization capture or buy, and how will you use it to motivate consumers to take action? How will you achieve personalization without invasion of privacy? How will you build intelligent automation without dehumanization?

Figuring out how to apply AI to your marketing may seem challenging now. But the real challenge, once you realize the power it gives you, is how to apply AI responsibly. As you think about your marketing AI strategy for the coming year, it's critical that you start to consider the implications, good and bad, of AI on your customers and other stakeholders.

Overestimated Responsible AI Practices

In a March 2021 report, BCG found that many large organizations overestimate their progress in implementing responsible AI programs, which BCG defines as "the structures, processes, and tools that help organizations ensure their AI systems work in the service of good while transforming their businesses."[94]

In the firm's analysis of more than one thousand organizations, BCG found that 55 percent of the companies were less advanced in their responsible AI journey than their senior executives believed. BCG analyzed seven generally accepted dimensions of responsible AI:

1. Accountability: Organizations and individuals designing, developing, deploying, or operating an AI system are responsible for the outcomes as well as for ensuring that they are used appropriately and effectively.

2. Transparency and Explainability: Organizations and individuals designing, developing, deploying, or operating an AI system must be transparent, explaining, as required, the purpose and goals of the system, how it was developed, and how outcomes are reached.

3. Fairness and Equity: AI systems are designed to be inclusive, to identify and mitigate sources of bias, and to promote fair outcomes.

4. Safety, Security, and Robustness: AI systems are designed to be secure and resilient and to have safeguards that reduce the risk of unintended behaviors and outcomes.

5. Data and Privacy Governance: AI systems are designed, and policies are in place, to ensure compliance with data privacy laws and to mitigate privacy risks.

6. Social and Environmental Impact Mitigation: AI systems are designed to promote positive, sustainable impact and to avoid creating or perpetuating adverse effects on society and the environment.

7. Human Plus AI: AI systems are designed to empower people (those who are developing, deploying, and using the systems), to preserve their authority over the systems, and to safeguard their well-being.

This study highlights the challenges that organizations of all sizes face as they look to scale the use of AI. It also brings into focus that responsible AI can be subjective.

While professionals can generally agree that responsible AI implies using the technology in ethical and transparent ways that do no harm, there will always be others who believe that as long as they stay within the laws and regulations that govern its use, they have more leeway to push the limits of what the technology enables. This can lead to both intentional and unintentional prioritization of revenue and growth over human-centered AI solutions.

Organizations Focused on Responsible AI

As your company looks to scale AI, you will want to stay up to date on the latest research and advancements in responsible AI. Here is a collection of organizations that are leading the way:

AI4ALL

AI4ALL (www.ai-4-all.org) is a US-based nonprofit dedicated to increasing diversity and inclusion in AI education, research, development, and policy. AI4ALL opens doors to artificial intelligence for historically excluded talent through education and mentorship. The organization believes that diverse perspectives, voices, and experiences unlock AI's potential to benefit humanity.

AI Now Institute

The AI Now Institute (www.ainowinstitute.org) at New York University is an interdisciplinary research center dedicated to understanding the social implications of artificial intelligence. The organization's work focuses on four core domains: rights and liberties, labor and automation, bias and inclusion, and safety and critical infrastructure.

Allen Institute for AI (AI2)

AI2 (www.allenai.org) is a nonprofit research institute founded in 2014 with the mission of conducting high-impact AI research and engineering in service of the common good. AI2 is the creation of Paul Allen, Microsoft cofounder, and is led by Dr. Oren Etzioni, a leading AI researcher.

Institute for Human-Centered AI (HAI)

The Stanford Institute for Human-Centered Artificial Intelligence (HAI) (hai.stanford.edu) was founded in early 2019 to guide and build the future of AI. The organization's mission is to advance AI research, education, policy, and practice to improve the human condition. Research focuses on developing AI technologies inspired by human intelligence; studying, forecasting, and guiding the human and societal impact of AI; and designing and creating AI applications that augment human capabilities.

Partnership on AI (PAI)

Adobe and Google are among more than one hundred members of the Partnership on AI (PAI) (www.partnershiponai.org), which was established in 2016 to study and formulate best practices on AI technologies, to advance the public's understanding of AI, and to serve as an open platform for discussion and engagement about AI and its influences on people and society.

PAI has six thematic pillars: safety-critical AI; fair, transparent, and accountable AI; AI, labor, and the economy; collaborations between people and AI systems; social and societal influences of AI; and AI and social good.

Women in AI (WAI)

Women in AI (www.womeninai.co) is a nonprofit working toward gender-inclusive AI that benefits global society. The organization's mission is to increase female representation and participation in AI through community building, blogging, events, and research.

More Intelligent. More Human.

In chapter fifteen, we ended with the idea of using AI as a vehicle to become a more human brand. But what does that really mean? In short, it means that rather than thinking of AI as a means to cut costs, reduce staff, and increase profits, leaders see AI as a way to redistribute resources and invest in their customers, employees, and communities; to build purpose-driven businesses that put people over profits.

These organizations seamlessly integrate AI with human capabilities and reinvest the time and money saved from intelligent automation into listening, relationship building, creativity, culture, and communities. This enables the brand and its leaders and employees to develop more rewarding connections through human-to-human interactions.

For consumers, human-centered AI delivers personalization and convenience in an unbiased and inclusive manner that respects individuality and privacy. AI removes friction from customer interactions and creates memorable and meaningful brand experiences.

For employees, human-centered AI removes repetitive, mundane tasks. It frees professionals to focus on more fulfilling and uniquely human skills and traits, such as common sense, compassion, creativity, curiosity, emotion, empathy, imagination, intuition, love, and strategy.

To bring this idea of "more intelligent, more human" to life, I like to start strategy documents with a simple outline of how we will apply the concept to solving problems and achieving goals. For example, here is an excerpt from a marketing strategy for MAICON ticket sales:

More Intelligent

- Forecast MAICON sales based on explicit and implicit data
- Predict high-priority contacts based on probability to purchase
- Drive efficiency in marketing resource allocation (time and money) through more targeted campaigns

More Human

- Understand individual learning paths, journeys, and needs
- Prioritize contacts for one-to-one engagement, nurturing, and community building
- Personalize messages, experiences, and marketing at scale
- Focus team on strategy and creativity, while investing significant resources in interpersonal communications with our audiences

This approach serves as a reference point throughout the strategic process, and a reminder to always keep human impact at the center of our planning.

What Makes Us Human and Separates Us From Machines?

In *AI Superpowers: China, Silicon Valley and the New World Order*,[95] author Kai-Fu Lee, a leading AI researcher, investor, and former president of Google China, shared a personal story about his battle with cancer and how it changed his perspective on AI.

Lee had spent his career driven by what he termed an almost fanatical work ethic, with his sense of self-worth being derived by his work achievements and his ability to create economic value and expand his influence in the world. The personal outcomes that he sought were often realized through his research career, working to build more powerful AI algorithms.

Then in 2013, he was diagnosed with stage IV lymphoma. He would go into remission, but the experience transformed how he viewed AI and how humans could coexist with the technology. He wrote that while AI will create massive economic value, he believed it will also destroy "an astounding number of jobs."[96] Lee warned that we cannot succeed in a future in which society judges the worth of human beings on the economic value they can create. He wrote that "there is another path, an opportunity to use artificial intelligence to double down on what makes us truly human. This path won't be easy, but I believe it represents our best hope of not just surviving in the age of AI but actually thriving."[97]

What Lee never realized during his time as a top AI researcher at the forefront of human knowledge about AI was that the one thing he could not give to or learn from algorithms was a true understanding of what makes us human and separates us from machines: the ability to love. It became his belief that by marrying the machine's ability to think with our human ability to love, we could "harness the undeniable power of artificial intelligence to generate prosperity while also embracing our essential humanity."[98]

To be more human means that as brands and marketers, learners and leaders, we must first accept that AI will transform the fabric of business and society at an accelerating rate. That is a fait accompli, an accomplished fact. It is nonnegotiable. But we have a choice about what we do next.

I live every day in between two realities. A marketer obsessed with AI, staring down the inevitable future of intelligent automation that will transform our industry, workforce, economy, and world, and that of a father, raising two amazing kids whose innocence, imagination, and creativity inspire me to demand more out of humanity. I want to help create a better world for them; to somehow find a balance that enables them, and the generations who come after them, to live better lives as consumers and as people.

I have to understand AI because I believe it will change society like nothing we have ever experienced before. But if we are thoughtful and intentional in how we use it, we can open up a whole new world of possibilities for our industry and beyond. If we can amplify the skills and traits that remain uniquely human and we use AI for the good of society, then the potential for AI is infinite.

We can teach machines to be like humans. We can tell them what to predict, and we can decide what to do with those predictions. We can give them the ability to see, hear, speak, move, write, and even in some capacity, understand. But we cannot make them human, and we must never forget that. We are not trying to replace humans. We are trying to unlock our true potential.

Being an AI pioneer comes with great responsibility. By providing personalization without invasion of privacy and intelligent automation without dehumanization, we can make marketing more intelligent and brands more human. The future is marketer plus machine. And the future is now.

Chapter 17

AI and You

The primary reason I founded Marketing AI Institute and eventually wrote this book was because I believed there was a story to tell. A story about the opportunity and uncertainty AI presents to the marketing industry and business world in general and individual careers in particular, as intelligent automation alters the knowledge and skill sets needed for success.

The number one question I get when giving AI presentations is, "Will it take my job?" I tend to focus on what I believe will be the net positive effect of AI, a symbiotic relationship between humans and machines. The machines will do all the data-driven, time-intensive work most humans don't enjoy anyway, while the humans spend their days being strategic, creative, empathetic, and, well, happier. But the reality is I have no idea what comes next. No one does.

I do know that the change is accelerating. While most marketers chalk up AI to the next overhyped technology, the unforgiving truth is that this technology transformation will be very different from anything that has come before. So what does AI mean for you?

For college students reading this, know that you will be entering the professional world at a time of unprecedented change. AI is rede-fining what is possible. The skills and knowledge you need to succeed will continually evolve at an increasingly rapid pace. Your education will give you the foundation you need to get started, but your commitment to being a lifelong learner is what will set you apart and present you a path to a fulfilling career. Don't be overwhelmed or afraid of AI. None of us truly knows what comes next. The opportunities before you, working with intelligent machines, are unparalleled in history. Let your curiosity guide you and never stop exploring.

For practitioners, this is not the same marketing industry we came into or grew up in. Whether you are early in your career, with aspirations to someday leave your mark on the business world; somewhere in the middle, still in search of your true career path while trying to find peace and balance along the way; or on the back end of your journey, looking to leave your legacy or maybe just leave things a little better than you found them, AI will affect every aspect of your career and life. I hope that you choose to embrace it and use it for good.

And for the leaders, directors, VPs, and CMOs, who this generation—and the next—look to for guidance, you have spent a career fighting an uphill battle of ever-changing priorities and technologies, moving from one chapter of digital transformation to the next. Some of you were in marketing when the internet and email took the world by storm. Most of you have witnessed the rise of social media, consumer-generated content, and the smartphone. And now comes the next frontier in digital transformation, the age of AI.

For everyone, know that consumer expectations, marketing, business, and society have changed forever. The best practices and industry benchmarks that have helped define our strategies and goals over the last two decades are irrelevant. Anything is possible now. Your future is whatever you want it to be. You get to write your own story of how AI will impact you and your career.

You can sit back and wait, put off understanding and adopting AI for the next month, quarter, or year. I would understand because it is abstract, and you have a million other things to do and worry about. But AI and the exponential growth it enables will not wait for you. The pace of innovation is unforgiving. The first movers, the pioneers, will struggle in the early going, but they will learn and so will the machines. That learning will compound over time, and your peers who take the initiative now will leave you behind.

The choice is yours.

You don't need to know how to build machine-learning models, and you don't need to know the technical details of how deep learning and neural networks work. But you do need to have a high level of competency in what AI is and what it is capable of doing. This knowledge gives you an ability to look at problems differently, the confidence to know when you have a viable use case, and the savvy to find and evaluate smarter marketing technology solutions.

Find the elements of AI that inspire you. Discover ways to intelligently automate repetitive tasks with machines, and reimagine how to build a fulfilling career by focusing on what remains, for the foreseeable future, uniquely human.

Rather than getting caught up in whether an intelligent machine is going to take your job or if it is going to handle tasks that you enjoy, step back and think about what opportunities are about to emerge. Consider what career paths may be opening, how you can help your business look beyond what we know today, and figure out what this is all going to look like tomorrow. You can become the change agent within your business and be the one who drives the next frontier in digital transformation.

Those who can imagine anything can create the impossible.
—Alan Turing, mathematician and AI pioneer

CONCLUSION

As humans, we're really good at thinking in a linear path. We can predict what tomorrow will be like with reasonable accuracy because it's logical to assume it will look and feel a lot like today. If you were to think about the year ahead and consider how you will do your job, who you will hire, how you will train them, what technology you will use, and what strategies you will employ, you would likely draw on your recent experiences and make assumptions based on what you've done in the past. You will tap into what is known and familiar to plan for the future. If, like many organizations, you also strategize for a three- to five-year outlook, in a similar way you would make predictions and build plans based on your existing knowledge and technologies. But what if the near future looks nothing like the recent past?

In 2001, Ray Kurzweil, a pioneering inventor, best-selling author, and futurist, wrote this:

> *An analysis of the history of technology shows that technological change is exponential, contrary to the common-sense "intuitive linear" view. So we won't experience 100 years of progress in the 21st century—it will be more like 20,000 years of progress (at today's rate). The "returns," such as chip speed and cost-effectiveness, also increase exponentially. There's even exponential growth in the rate of exponential growth. Within a few decades, machine intelligence will surpass human intelligence, leading to The Singularity—technological change so rapid and profound it*

represents a rupture in the fabric of human history. The implications
include the merger of biological and nonbiological intelligence, immortal
software-based humans, and ultra-high levels of intelligence that expand
outward in the universe at the speed of light.[99]

Kurzweil's views on the inevitable singularity—the point in time at which machines are smarter than humans—and how close we are to achieving it (he predicts by 2045) are commonly debated. But there's no denying his core assumption that the pace of change is accelerating at a rate that will be increasingly difficult for our human minds to comprehend.

So what can you do when so much about the future is unknown? You have three options:

1. Maintain the Status Quo: Continue going about your career as though nothing is changing, when, in reality, everything is changing. This is the easiest path in the short term, but also the fastest route to becoming obsolete.
2. Work Harder: Put in more hours in an effort to keep pace. This may work for a short period, but eventually technology will pass you by, and you will have sacrificed precious time with family and friends along the way.
3. Work Smarter: Lead the charge within your organization to adopt AI-powered technology that constantly learns and improves. The result is that you achieve more while working less. With this option, you are able to redistribute your time to more fulfilling activities in your career, and you find more freedom to invest energy in the things and people that matter in your personal life.

The reality is that option three is the only viable path. The future is exponential. Technological change will come in waves that will make the current ways of doing things seem elementary. But you now have the knowledge needed to take action. You can future-proof your career by becoming a next-gen marketer. Don't wait for the marketing world to get smarter around you. Take the initiative to understand, pilot, and scale AI.

Twelve Things to Know About Artificial Intelligence

Here are key takeaways that reinforce important points from throughout the book:

1. Your life is already AI assisted, and your marketing will be, too.
2. Artificial intelligence is the science of making *machines* smart. Marketing artificial intelligence is the science of making *marketing* smart.
3. Machine learning is the primary subset of AI. Deep learning is a subset of machine learning.
4. AI enhances human knowledge and capabilities. The future is marketer plus machine.
5. AI reduces costs by intelligently automating repetitive, data-driven tasks.
6. AI drives revenue by improving your ability to make predictions.
7. AI powers smarter technology that solves problems and achieves goals more efficiently than traditional marketing technology.
8. Consumers demand greater personalization while controlling their data and privacy.
9. AI gives marketers and brands superpowers, which can be used for good or for evil.
10. AI has the potential to make brands more human.
11. AI adoption in marketing is still in its early stages.
12. AI can be your competitive advantage.

The following section contains highlights from each chapter.

Chapter Highlights

Chapter 1: The Science of Making Marketing Smart

- Think about how rapidly technology has evolved over the last two decades. Now imagine that multiplied by a factor of ten, twenty, or even one hundred. That is the challenge AI presents. It is accelerating the velocity of change.
- AI is forecasted to have trillions of dollars of impact on businesses and the economy, yet the majority of marketers struggle to understand what it is and how to apply it to their marketing.
- *AI* is the umbrella term for the algorithms, technologies, and techniques that make machines smart and give marketers superhuman capabilities.
- The most important element of machine learning, and what truly differentiates it from traditional statistics and computer science, is that it continues to evolve and improve based on new data. In other words, it gets smarter.
- Deep learning is a subset of machine learning. In a simplified way of explaining it, deep learning takes different approaches to emulating how the human brain learns and works in order to give machines the ability to see, hear, speak, write, move, and understand.
- Much of the deep-learning story has unfolded over the last ten years as the technology began to move from decades of academic theory and false hopes into practical commercial applications across industries.
- Major technology companies are in a race for AI talent and supremacy, largely fueled by the potential for deep learning to transform the future of business. You see deep learning at work in search results, voice assistants, text generation, translation, facial and image recognition, and hundreds of other consumer-facing technologies.

Chapter 2: Language, Vision, and Prediction

- The three broad categories of AI are language, vision, and prediction. Within those categories are dozens of AI applications that can be used to make your marketing smarter. And within those dozens of AI applications are thousands of use cases that can drive efficiency and performance in your business.

- Language is the ability for machines to understand and generate written and spoken words.

- To understand the potential power of AI in this category, think of all the ways language plays a role in basically any marketing function that has to do with writing, speaking, and listening. Now imagine that a machine could intelligently automate or augment all your daily tasks and marketing programs in which language is analyzed or generated.

- There is a race to train AI systems to generate human language at scale. When achieved, the implications, both good and bad, are immense.

- Vision is the ability for machines to analyze and understand data from images and videos.

- You experience the convenience of vision applications every day when you unlock devices using facial recognition, share GIFs that have been automatically tagged with image recognition, and discover recommended videos on social media thanks to video recognition.

- Prediction is the ability for machines to forecast future outcomes based on historical data.

- With machine learning, predictions continually evolve and improve based on new data. The better the data that goes in (the inputs), the better the predictions that come out (the outputs). Prediction is probably the most relevant category to you right now, as it has the potential to improve your decision-making across every area of marketing and business.

Chapter 3: The Marketer-to-Machine Scale

- We are years away from AI being seamlessly infused into every marketing technology, but you can buy smarter solutions today for specific use cases that will help your organization reduce costs and accelerate revenue. You just need to know how to find and assess AI technology.

- When you are buying AI-powered technology, it's critical to remember that AI does not replace you; it augments your knowledge and capabilities to different degrees. In essence, you are trying to determine what the machine will do and what the marketer will do.

- The Marketer-to-Machine (M2M) Scale classifies five levels of intelligent automation at the use case level. It's not trying to rate an entire company or platform but a specific AI technology for a narrowly defined application or task.

- By understanding which M2M level a technology enables, you are better able to determine how it will impact your business, your team, and the full scope of work required to adopt and scale it.

- A little bit of AI can go a long way in reducing costs and driving revenue when you have the right data and use cases. You don't need to go from fully manual to fully autonomous to see massive returns.

- Much of the marketing technology you use today is Level 0, all human, all the time. You plan and execute everything, and the software does what you tell it to do. The software does not learn, it does not improve, and it does not make you better at your job.

- Most AI-powered marketing solutions available today have some basic to moderate levels of intelligent automation and fit into Levels 1 and 2. Level 3 is possible but only after a significant investment of time and inputs during planning, training, and onboarding phases. Level 4 does not exist in marketing today.

- AI needs information, or inputs, to learn and perform its tasks. Inputs commonly are in the form of structured or unstructured data that the human provides to the machine.
- Oversight is the level of training, monitoring, and intervention the machine needs.
- Dependence is how reliant the machine is on the marketer to complete its objective.
- Improvement is the process by which the machine learns and improves.
- AI is just smarter marketing technology. But it's what you should be demanding from the vendors in your tech stack.
- The more you understand AI and what to look for in solutions, the greater chance you have of finding the right technologies that create value for your company.

Chapter 4: Getting Started with Marketing AI

- The 5Ps of Marketing AI is a beta framework to help visualize and organize the marketing AI technology landscape.
- The 5Ps are as follows:
  - Planning: Building intelligent strategies
  - Production: Creating intelligent content
  - Personalization: Powering intelligent consumer experiences
  - Promotion: Managing intelligent cross-channel promotions
  - Performance: Turning data into intelligence
- AI Score for Marketers (score.marketingaiinstitute.com) is a free online assessment tool that enables you to explore and rate dozens of AI use cases and get personalized recommendations for AI-powered vendors.
- It's important to remember that use cases are subjective. Since AI Score lets each individual rank the use cases based on their own perceived value to intelligently automate a task, a low-ranked use case for one marketer may have the potential to unlock enormous value for others.

- When you are getting started with AI and looking to build internal support, you will want to focus your investments on quick-win pilot projects with narrowly defined scopes and high probabilities of success. Specifically, you are looking for use cases that are data driven, repetitive, and predictive.
- Starting with use cases is the fastest way to pilot AI and create efficiencies in your marketing. But the problem-based model will likely have the greater long-term impact on enterprise value. In this model, you have a known pain point or a challenge that may be solved more efficiently and at scale with AI.
- Piloting and scaling AI goes well beyond finding a few use cases and vendors. AI will fundamentally transform your talent, technology, and strategy in the months and years to come.

Chapter 5: Advertising and AI

- Consumers control what they choose to read, view, listen to, and pay attention to, and they have unlimited power to "change the channel" if they aren't being served in the way they want.
- Advertisers now must compete for seconds or milliseconds of fragmented consumer attention across millions of digital destinations, apps, and experiences in real time.
- AI-powered technology enables advertisers to reach more of the right people in the right moments for much less than it would have cost decades ago to buy a billboard or create a television commercial.
- Creating, targeting, and optimizing modern ads effectively is simply too complex a task for human advertisers to do well.
- The story is still unfolding as of this writing, but the third-party cookie and user-tracking infrastructure that powers today's advertising seems to be under threat.
- These sea changes to the industry mean first-party data is more important than ever. Without first-party data, marketers will

be at the mercy of the few companies (like Google) that end up owning consumer data in a post-cookie world.

Chapter 6: Analytics and AI

- AI excels at analyzing large datasets, providing analytics that tell you not only what's happening now, but also what you should do about it.
- AI-powered analytics tools find patterns within large datasets, then predict future patterns using what it learned. It's increasingly used by brands because of one simple fact: we now have too much data.
- Marketers have the ability to unleash AI-powered analytics across marketing organizations to extract insights at scale.
- AI-powered analytics tools are helping marketers and brands win in three significant ways:
  1. Increase revenue by analyzing and acting on data at scale
  2. Reduce costs by acting on that data faster and automatically
  3. Build a massive competitive advantage with both superior insights and superior speed

Chapter 7: Communications, PR, and AI

- With the power of AI, brands have unlocked new ways to create and distribute their messages, protect and enhance their reputations, and inspire legions of raving fans.
- PR and communications professionals using the technology have discovered new ways to reach and influence consumers at scale.
- AI can enhance what you already do by providing greater insights and expanded data on what works with audiences, outlets, and messaging; making creation and distribution easier, faster, and more scalable; and automating tedious,

time-consuming tasks that take you away from the high-impact creative work you, your bosses, and your clients love.

- Forward-thinking brands are using AI to automatically create messages that resonate, design brand collateral tested against millions of top examples, and tap into vast dataflows that reveal consumer sentiment in real time to shape brand perceptions.

Chapter 8: Content Marketing and AI

- AI can already read and write human language, and every time AI systems read and write, they learn a little more about how to read and write better.
- The benefits of using AI are apparent. It increases revenue by giving you accurate, data-driven recommendations on content that works, and it decreases costs by reducing the time, waste, and effort needed to create and promote content.
- AI is skilled at partially or fully producing content, promoting it, and predicting content performance, and it's already being adopted by brands to build a competitive content advantage.
- Machines can—and will—take over some content tasks historically done by humans. As this happens, brands will increasingly place value on humans who can do strategic and creative work.
- You can build a smarter content strategy from the ground up using AI.

Chapter 9: Customer Service and AI

- The new normal means consumers demand always-on self-directed service and experiences, and failing to deliver has serious consequences.

- Conversational AI is automatic, scalable, and you can calibrate it to be empathetic and engaging to humans. So adopting AI is a no-brainer for brands flooded with online customer requests.
- Brands now use AI to extract insights from customer data generated by calls and messages. They use these insights to create better, more personalized experiences.
- Brands also deploy AI to detect content and sentiment on customer service calls, then route calls to an agent at the right time. That allows them to pinpoint the moment customers are frustrated or confused, then step in to help at the right time.
- The pandemic forced companies to offer customer service digitally. But even when COVID-19 is a distant memory, we're not going back. This change has been a long time coming because it's fundamentally driven by changing consumer expectations.

Chapter 10: Ecommerce and AI

- Ecommerce was already eating the business world before COVID-19, but the pandemic poured gasoline on the fire.
- As a survival mechanism, ecommerce marketers embraced AI-powered technology. Conversational agents and bots became essential to handle sales and support. Recommendation and discovery were critical to generate sales during entirely self-directed customer journeys. And forecasting was mandatory to stay stocked amid unprecedented demand.
- Amazon possesses a potentially insurmountable advantage in AI for ecommerce. It has some of the best algorithms, talent, and computing power—thanks to AWS and massive investments in computing infrastructure—and more data on consumer purchases and habits than almost any other company on Earth.
- Early AI adoption has created a flywheel effect at Amazon. The smarter its AI gets, the more it sells. The more it sells, the more data it collects. The more data it collects, the smarter its AI gets.

Chapter 11: Email Marketing and AI

- AI isn't just for writing subject lines, though it's excellent at that. It can also evaluate your database to make sure it's healthy and valid. It can use email validation to make sure your emails actually land in the recipient's inbox. And it can help you segment lists so you deliver more relevant offers to your valuable customers.
- AI handles complexity we can't. Human marketers can't monitor and react to algorithmic changes in the filters used by email clients. We can't efficiently clean up lists so that our emails go to the right people, especially in large databases. We can't do advanced list segmentation. We can't even consistently create email copy that customers and prospects love.
- AI is an email marketer's new best friend. It makes sense of your data so you can base campaign decisions on math. It can optimize your campaigns and put more money in your pocket. In some cases, it can even contact prospects for you.
- You don't need a PhD to discover and use AI solutions. You need a list of problems to solve and the curiosity to research further. There's a decent chance your problems are related to human limitations, a good chance technology exists to help, and a great chance that AI powers that technology.

Chapter 12: Sales and AI

- AI in sales isn't about replacing seasoned salespeople at all. It's about helping seasoned salespeople sell more.
- AI excels at taking sales data and using it to make better predictions and recommendations than humans can on their own.
- While traditional software uses simple rules-based automation to streamline work, AI finds insights, opportunities, and patterns that traditional software can't.

- AI can detect churn signals in real time, predict which leads will close, and find new leads that match your ideal prospects.

Chapter 13: SEO and AI

- Search engines now use advanced algorithms to serve consumers the most relevant search results across devices, employ machine learning and NLP to predict search intent and match results to it, and take into account user behaviors and interactions across text and voice platforms.
- Google uses many algorithms to serve a single search result. These algorithms don't just read what you type. They understand what you say (in text or out loud); take into account your location and settings; parse hundreds of billions of pages in a search index; use many factors to judge the authority, usability, quality, and relevance of all web pages providing possible answers; and serve the best results.
- Thanks to pattern recognition, AI can identify trends and insights in search data that humans can't. And with NLU, AI can understand the intent behind searches. These capabilities give brands several compelling use cases for AI in SEO.
- AI makes Alexa, Siri, and other voice assistants possible in the first place. NLP and NLG make sure voice assistants offer accurate, understandable, and helpful responses.

Chapter 14: Social Media Marketing and AI

- Any social media platform you use today, either as a consumer or a marketer, relies heavily on AI to serve content to users, determine what content will keep users on the platform, and suggest additional content to keep them coming back.
- Perhaps paradoxically, the solution to perform well on social media platforms that rely on AI is to use more AI, to fight

machines with more machines that can offer a brand unique advantages when it comes to performance—and protection—on social media.

- AI-powered social media tools can use data to predict which posts will work, create posts automatically, detect consumer trends that humans can't, and moderate comments.
- Consumer behavior dictates that brands engage with consumers in a personalized, helpful, and authentic way on social media channels, building real communities and relationships around shared interests and topics.
- Brands may be tempted to use manipulative messaging and incendiary content to capture attention. They may even be temporarily rewarded for it by social media algorithms. But in the long term, such behaviors damage brand equity and harm society. Done often enough, they destroy consumer trust and negatively impact mental and physical health.

Chapter 15: Scaling AI

- Industries in which there are frequent digital interactions with consumers will see the greatest potential for returns from AI. These regular interactions through websites, emails, mobile apps, voice assistants, and Internet of Things devices create larger data sets based on behavior and intent signals that can be used to continually train and improve AI applications.
- AI will accelerate your ability to create and personalize content and experiences at scale. Machines can create, and they can inspire human creativity. The value that can be unlocked as a result is immense.
- The financial reward for successfully scaling AI is significant, but the reality is that most businesses are still in the infancy of AI adoption.
- The learning curve and costs associated with deploying AI technology serve as barriers to entry for many leaders and

businesses. As these subside and the technology becomes more prevalent and easier to apply, AI's contribution to growth and value within enterprises will rapidly accelerate.

- The window of opportunity to seize an early mover advantage is short. You have to act now to put AI at the foundation of your marketing talent, technology, and strategy.
- Next-gen marketers consider the ramifications of the AI technology they create and use. AI will have a disproportionate net positive impact on the industry and society, but it will alter career paths, displace jobs, and continually chip away at our privacy as consumers.

Chapter 16: More Human

- Any time you have a race to lead the advancement of a technology like AI, there are people and companies who push forward and challenge what is accepted as normal and ethical.
- The value exchange between consumers (data) and tech companies (personalization) is what powers many of the AI innovations that are changing our lives.
- You need to address bias at every step of a process that leads to the adoption of AI in products and operations.
- An excellent way to start building and using AI for good is to draft an AI ethics policy for your organization. An AI ethics statement is a formal document posted publicly that outlines your company's position on AI. It provides specifics on how your company will and won't use AI.
- With AI, we can learn more about consumers than ever before. We can discover their beliefs, interests, fears, and desires. We can use that information to manipulate consumers. We can make predictions about their behavior and then trigger those behaviors in ways that are unethical.
- The real challenge, once you realize the power it gives you, is how to apply AI responsibly.

- Rather than thinking of AI as a means to cut costs, reduce staff, and increase profits, leaders see AI as a way to redistribute resources and invest in their customers, employees, and communities; to build purpose-driven businesses that put people over profits.
- Being an AI pioneer comes with great responsibility: personalization without invasion of privacy; intelligent automation without dehumanization. We can make marketing more intelligent, and brands more human.

Chapter 17: AI and You

- While most marketers chalk up AI to the next overhyped technology, the unforgiving truth is that this technology transformation will be different from anything that has come before.
- Consumer expectations, marketing, business, and society have changed forever.
- AI, and the exponential growth it will enable, will not wait for you. The pace of innovation is unforgiving.
- You need to have a high level of competency in what AI is and what it is capable of doing. This knowledge gives you an ability to look at problems differently, the confidence to know when you have a viable use case, and the savvy to find and evaluate smarter marketing technology solutions.

ACKNOWLEDGMENTS

In late 2021, as we were finishing the manuscript for this book, we announced that we were setting out on an educational journey to introduce AI to one million marketers by the end of 2026.

Why?

Because AI is changing the industry, the economy, society, and your career, and not nearly enough marketers and business leaders have even a baseline understanding of the technology.

One million is 10 percent of the approximately 10 million global marketers, which seems possible to reach through content, webinars, conferences, podcasts, reports, interactive tools, and online courses—especially with the help of our partner universities, vendors, and associations.

Our hypothesis is that we can spark enough curiosity in those one million to get 10 percent, or one hundred thousand, to take the next step (e.g., listen to an AI podcast, read a book, take an online course, demo an AI technology, attend a conference, subscribe to an AI newsletter, etc.).

Then we can turn 10 percent of those, or ten thousand people, into a community of next-gen marketers who join forces to create a movement. Together, we reinvent what it means to be a marketer, build smarter brands, and make marketing more human (think "AI for good").

But none of what we've done to date, or where we hope to go in the future, is possible without our people:

- Our MAICON attendees, AI Academy for Marketers learners, newsletter subscribers, and community members who motivate us to create content that educates and inspires.
- Our MAICON speakers and AI Academy for Marketers instructors who so graciously share their time and expertise with our audiences.
- Our sponsors who have provided financial and promotional support since day one.
- Our investors who believed in a vision to transform an industry through education.
- Our business partners who make it possible for us to run a world-class conference (special thanks to Kelley Whetsell, Ashlee Moehring, and the Meeting Demands team), and build a next-generation media, event, and education company.
- Our PR 20/20 and Marketing AI Institute teams who brought our business to life and have powered its growth since 2016.

Thank you!

ENDNOTES

Chapter 1

1   Christopher Steiner, *Automate This: How Algorithms Took Over Our Markets, Our Jobs and Our World* (New York: Penguin Group, 2012), 119.

2   Steiner, *Automate This*, 7.

3   Sam Altman, "Moore's Law for Everything" (blog), https://moores .samaltman.com.

4   "2021 State of Marketing AI Report," Marketing AI Institute and Drift, January 2021, www.stateofmarketingai.com.

5   Mark Cuban, Twitter post, January 23, 2021, 2:24 PM, https://twitter.com/ mcuban/status/1353061068780658690.

6   Mark Cuban, Twitter post, January 23, 2021, 9:11 AM, https://twitter.com/ mcuban/status/1352982281514864640.

7   "Jeff Bezos vs Peter Thiel and Donald Trump | Jeff Bezos, CEO Amazon | Code Conference 2016," YouTube video, 4:08, posted by "Recode," June 1, 2016, https://youtu.be/guVxubbQQKE.

8   Jordan Novet, "Amazon Web Services tops analysts' estimates on profit and revenue," *CNBC*, October 28, 2021, https://www.cnbc.com/2021/10/28/aws -earnings-q3-2021.html.

9   Sean Hollister, "Google just had another record quarter because or in spite of everything going on," *The Verge*, October 26, 2021, https://www.theverge .com/2021/10/26/22747193/google-q3-2021-earnings-record-revenue-profit.

10   "Machine Learning on AWS," Amazon AWS Home Page, June 10, 2021, https://aws.amazon.com/machine-learning/.

11   "AWS for Marketers," Amazon AWS Industry Page, Sept. 15, 2021, https://aws.amazon.com/advertising-marketing/aws-for-marketers/.

12   John Batelle, "The Birth of Google," *Wired*, August 1, 2005, https://www.wired.com/2005/08/battelle/.

13   Sergey Brin and Lawrence Page, "The Anatomy of a Large-Scale Hypertextual Web Search Engine," Stanford University InfoLab, April 1998, http://infolab.stanford.edu/~backrub/google.html.

14   Spencer Michels, "Google: The Search Engine that Could," PBS NewsHour, Nov. 29, 2002, https://www.pbs.org/newshour/show/google-the-search-engine-that-could.

15   Sergey Brin, "2017 Founders' Letter," Alphabet Investor Relations, https://abc.xyz/investor/founders-letters/2017/index.html.

16   Sundar Pichai, "2018 Founders' Letter," Alphabet Investor Relations, https://abc.xyz/investor/founders-letters/2018/.

17   Pichai, "2018 Founders' Letter."

18   "Sundar Pichai: AI will have greater impact than electricity | Forum Insight," YouTube video, 0:00, posted by World Economic Forum, December 6, 2019, https://youtu.be/OXcJw5tW9RY.

19   "AI and machine learning products," Google Cloud Page, March 21, 2021, https://cloud.google.com/products/ai.

20   Jeff Dean, "Bringing the benefits of AI to everyone," Google AI About Page, March 21, 2021, https://ai.google/about/.

21   Stuart Zweben, "Record Ph.D. Production on the Horizon; Undergraduate Enrollments Continue in Decline," Computing Research Association Archive, May 2005, https://archive.cra.org/CRN/articles/may05/taulbee.html.

22   Steve Lohr, "Microsoft, Amid Dwindling Interest, Talks Up Computing as a Career," *New York Times*, March 1, 2004, https://www.nytimes.com/2004/03/01/business/microsoft-amid-dwindling-interest-talks-up-computing-as-a-career.html.

23   Guy Berger, "The Jobs of Tomorrow: LinkedIn's 2020 Emerging Jobs Report," LinkedIn Official Blog, December 10, 2019, https://blog.linkedin.com/2019/december/10/the-jobs-of-tomorrow-linkedins-2020-emerging-jobs-report.

24   Matt Clinch and Natasha Turak, "Microsoft CEO Satya Nadella on the rise
      of A.I.: 'The future we will invent is a choice we make'," CNBC Tech Page,
      May 24, 2018, https://www.cnbc.com/2018/05/24/microsoft-ceo-satya
      -nadella-on-the-rise-of-a-i-the-future-we-will-invent-is-a-choice-we-make
      .html.

25   "AI-first approach across industries will transform us: Microsoft CEO Satya
      Nadella," *Statesman*, July 19, 2018, https://www.thestatesman.com
      /technology/ai-first-approach-across-industries-will-transform-us-microsoft
      -ceo-satya-nadella-1502662951.html.

26   "Satya Nadella: Microsoft Inspire 2018," Microsoft Leadership Page, July 18,
      2018, https://news.microsoft.com/speeches/satya-nadella-microsoft-inspire
      -2018/.

27   "Azure Cognitive Services," Microsoft Azure, accessed June 10, 2021, https://
      azure.microsoft.com/en-us/services/cognitive-services/.

Chapter 2

28   Ashley Pilipiszyn, "GPT-3 Powers the Next Generation of Apps," *OpenAI*
      (blog), March 25, 2021, https://openai.com/blog/gpt-3-apps/.

29   Dan, "Video recognition—The future of marketing and a 1st for social
      listening," *Talkwalker* (blog), March 19, 2019, https://www.talkwalker.com/
      blog/video-recognition-1st-social-listening.

30   Dami Lee, "Deepfake Salvador Dalí takes selfies with museum visitors,"
      Verge, May 10, 2019, https://www.theverge.com/platform/amp/2019/5/10
      /18540953/salvador-dali-lives-deepfake-museum.

31   Dalvin Brown, "Wait, is that video real? The race against deepfakes and
      dangers of manipulated recordings," *USA Today*, May 13, 2019, https://www
      .usatoday.com/story/tech/2019/05/13/deepfakes-why-your-instagram-photos
      -video-could-be-vulnerable/3344536002/.

32   Ajay Agrawal, Joshua Gans, and Avi Goldfarb, *Prediction Machines: The
      Simple Economics of Artificial Intelligence* (Boston: Harvard Business Review
      Press, 2018).

Chapter 3

33   Jennifer Shuttleworth, "SAE Standards News: J3016 automated-driving graphic update," SAE International, January 7, 2019, https://www.sae.org/news/2019/01/sae-updates-j3016-automated-driving-graphic.

34   Roberto Baldwin, "Tesla Tells California DMV that FSD Is Not Capable of Autonomous Driving," *Car and Driver*, March 9, 2021, https://www.caranddriver.com/news/a35785277/tesla-fsd-california-self-driving/.

35   Tesla, "Autopilot," Tesla, accessed June 10, 2021, https://www.tesla.com/autopilotAI.

Chapter 4

36   Sam Ransbotham, Philipp Gerbert, Martin Reeves, David Kiron, and Michael Spira, "Artificial Intelligence in Business Gets Real: Pioneering Companies Aim for AI at Scale," MIT Sloan Management Review, September 17, 2018, https://sloanreview.mit.edu/projects/artificial-intelligence-in-business-gets-real/.

Chapter 5

37   Mike Kaput, "How One Ecommerce Company Used AI to Get a 3,000% Return on Ad Spend," Marketing Artificial Intelligence Institute, November 30, 2018, https://www.marketingaiinstitute.com/blog/how-one-ecommerce-company-used-ai-to-get-a-3000-return-on-ad-spend.

38   Ibid.

39   Ibid.

40   Ibid.

41   "Programmatic's Share of Global Digital Display Ad Spend Expected to Keep Climbing," Marketing Charts, December 19, 2019, https://www.marketingcharts.com/advertising-trends/programmatic-and-rtb-111372.

42   "Top 5 Companies, Ranked by US Net Digital Ad Revenue Share, 2018 & 2019," Insider Intelligence, February 1, 2019, https://www.emarketer.com

/chart/226372/top-5-companies-ranked-by-us-net-digital-ad-revenue-share
-2018-2019-of-total-digital-ad-spending.

43 David Temkin, "Charting a course towards a more privacy-first web," *Google Ads* (blog), March 3, 2021, https://blog.google/products/ads-commerce
/a-more-privacy-first-web.

44 "IAB State of Data Initiative," IAB, March 11, 2021, https://www.iab.com/
insights/2021-iab-state-of-data.

45 Chris Kelly, "88% of marketers say collecting first-party data is a 2021
priority, study says," Marketing Dive, January 12, 2021, https://www
.marketingdive.com/news/88-of-marketers-say-collecting-first-party-data
-is-a-2021-priority-study/593174.

46 Mathew Sweezey, "The Post Cookie Future," September 29, 2020, https://
mathewsweezey.com/the-post-cookie-future.

Chapter 7

47 Joele Forrester, "CGI Influencer Lil Miquela Signs With Talent Agency
CAA," Talking Influence, May 15, 2020, https://talkinginfluence.com/2020
/05/07/cgi-influencer-lil-miquela-signs-caa.

Chapter 9

48 Sherry Chiger, "How Clorox Used AI and Chatbots for Customer Service
Inquiries During the Pandemic," Chief Marketer, April 15, 2021, https://
www.chiefmarketer.com/how-clorox-used-ai-and-chatbots-for-customer
-service-inquiries-during-the-pandemic.

49 Tom Puthiyamadam and José Reyes, "Experience Is Everything: Here's How
to Get It Right," PwC, accessed June 7, 2021, https://www.pwc.com/us/en/
services/consulting/library/consumer-intelligence-series/future-of-customer
-experience.html.

50 LaBerge et al., "How COVID-19 Has Pushed Companies over the Technology
Tipping Point—and Transformed Business Forever," McKinsey & Company,
October 5, 2020, https://www.mckinsey.com/business-functions/strategy

-and-corporate-finance/our-insights/how-covid-19-has-pushed-companies
-over-the-technology-tipping-point-and-transformed-business-forever.

51   Puthiyamadam and Reyes, "Experience is Everything: Here's How to Get It
Right."

52   "Customer Experience Trends Report 2021," Zendesk, accessed May 15,
2021, https://www.zendesk.com/cx-trends-report.

53   Ibid.

Chapter 10

54   "Pomelo Fashion Enhances Shoppers' Experience, Increases Revenue Using
Amazon Personalize," AWS, 2021, https://aws.amazon.com/solutions/
case-studies/pomelo-case-study.

55   "Customer Experience Trends Report 2021," Zendesk.

56   "Future of Commerce 2021," Shopify, accessed May 16, 2021, https://cdn
.shopify.com/static/future-of-commerce/Shopify%20Future%20of%20
Commerce%202021.pdf.

57   Ian MacKenzie, Chris Meyer, and Steve Noble, "How retailers can keep up
with consumers," McKinsey & Company, October 1, 2013, https://www
.mckinsey.com/industries/retail/our-insights/how-retailers-can-keep-up
-with-consumers.

58   Maryam Mohsin, "10 Email Marketing Stats You Need to Know in 2021
[Infographic]," Oberlo, June 1, 2020, https://www.oberlo.com/blog/
email-marketing-statistics.

59   Brian Dean, "57 Key Email Marketing Stats For 2021," Backlinko, January 28,
2021, https://backlinko.com/email-marketing-stats.

60   "The New Rules of Email Marketing," Campaign Monitor, accessed
May 16, 2021, https://www.campaignmonitor.com/resources/guides/
email-marketing-new-rules.

Chapter 12

61 "State of Sales, 3rd Edition," Salesforce, accessed May 1, 2021, https://www
.salesforce.com/form/conf/state-of-sales-3rd-edition.

Chapter 13

62 Camden Gaspar, "How to Boost Blog Traffic 1,570% (With Example),"
MarketMuse, April 16, 2021, https://blog.marketmuse.com/how-to-boost
-blog-traffic-1570-with-example.

63 Pandu Nayak, "MUM: A new AI milestone for understanding information,"
Google, May 18, 2021, https://blog.google/products/search/introducing
-mum.

64 Ibid.

65 James Moar and Meike Escherich, "Voice Assistants: Monetisation
Strategies, Competitive Landscape & Market Forecasts 2021-2026," Juniper
Research, February 8, 2021, https://www.juniperresearch.com/researchstore
/content-digital-media/voice-assistants-market-research-report.

66 Sandie Young, "AI Academy Instructors Explain How to Get Started
with Voice Strategy," Marketing Artificial Intelligence Institute,
February 11, 2021, https://www.marketingaiinstitute.com/blog/
ai-academy-instructors-explain-how-to-get-started-with-voice-strategy.

67 Ibid.

Chapter 14

68 Jim James, "The UnNoticed Entrepreneur—Public Relations for Business,"
Buzzsprout, September 25, 2020, https://www.buzzsprout.com/850540
/5605345.

69 "AI in Social Media Market Worth $2.197.1 Million by 2023," Marketsand-
Markets, accessed May 17, 2021, https://www.marketsandmarkets.com
/PressReleases/ai-in-social-media.asp.

70   Jeremy Kahn, "Can A.I. help Facebook cure its disinformation problem?" *Fortune*, April 6, 2021, https://fortune.com/2021/04/06/facebook -disinformation-ai-fake-news-us-capitol-attack-social-media-hate-speech -big-tech-solutions.

Chapter 15

71   Michael Chui et al., "Notes from the AI frontier: Applications and value of deep learning," McKinsey & Company, April 17, 2018, https://www.mckinsey.com/featured-insights/artificial-intelligence/ notes-from-the-ai-frontier-applications-and-value-of-deep-learning.

72   "Visualizing the uses and potential impact of AI and other analytics," McKinsey & Company, April 17, 2018, https:// www.mckinsey.com/featured-insights/artificial-intelligence/ visualizing-the-uses-and-potential-impact-of-ai-and-other-analytics.

73   Cade Metz, "In Two Moves, AlphaGo and Lee Sedol Redefined the Future," *Wired*, March 16, 2016, https://www.wired.com/2016/03/ two-moves-alphago-lee-sedol-redefined-future/.

74   "AlphaGo—The Movie | Full Documentary," YouTube video, posted by DeepMind, 51:12 – 51:16, March 13, 2020, https://youtu.be/WXuK6gekU1Y.

75   Ibid.

76   Ibid.

77   "2021 State of Marketing AI Report," Marketing AI Institute and Drift, January 2021, www.stateofmarketingai.com.

78   Nick Millman, "How to build a data strategy to scale AI," Accenture, May 15, 2020, https://www.accenture.com/us-en/insights/applied-intelligence/ build-data-strategy.

79   Andrew Ng, "AI Transformation Playbook: How to lead your company into the AI era," Landing AI, accessed June 10, 2021, https://landing.ai/ ai-transformation-playbook/.

80   Arielle Padres, "The Style-Quantifying Astrophysicists of Silicon Valley," *Wired*, October 7, 2019, https://www.wired.com/story/ the-style-maven-astrophysicists-of-silicon-valley/.

81   Mike Walsh, *The Algorithmic Leader: How to Be Smart When the Machines Are Smarter Than You* (Canada: Tomorrow, 2019), 55.

82   "2021 State of Marketing AI Report," Marketing AI Institute and Drift, January 2021, www.stateofmarketingai.com.

83   Ransbotham et al., "Artificial Intelligence in Business Gets Real: Pioneering Companies Aim for AI at Scale." September 17, 2018, https://sloanreview. mit.edu/projects/artificial-intelligence-in-business-gets-real/.

84   Joseph E. Aoun, *Robot-Proof: Higher Education in the Age of Artificial Intelligence* (Cambridge: The MIT Press, 2017).

85   NVIDIA, "It's Time for Colleges to Embrace Artificial Intelligence," The Chronicle of Higher Education, accessed June 10, 2021, https://sponsored .chronicle.com/it-s-time-for-colleges-to-embrace-artificial-intelligence/ index.html.

86   Ibid.

87   Ibid.

88   Sam Ransbotham et al., "Expanding AI's Impact with Organizational Learning," MIT Sloan Management Review, October 19, 2020, https:// sloanreview.mit.edu/projects/expanding-ais-impact-with-organizational -learning/.

Chapter 16

89   David Heinemeier Hansson, Twitter post, November 8, 2019, 3:29 pm, https://twitter.com/dhh/status/1192947185865785344.

90   "Taking an ethical approach to artificial intelligence," Adobe AI Ethics Page, accessed June 10, 2021, https://www.adobe.com/content/dam/cc/en/ ai-ethics/pdfs/Adobe-AI-Ethics-Principles.pdf.

91   Dana Rao, "Adobe unveils new AI ethics principles as part of commitment to responsible digital citizenship," *Adobe Blog*, February 17, 2021, https:// blog.adobe.com/en/publish/2021/02/17/adobe-unveils-new-ai-ethics -principles-commitment-responsible-digital-citizenship.html#gs.30m7bo.

92   "Artificial Intelligence at Google: Our Principles," Google AI Principles Page, accessed June 10, 2021, https://ai.google/principles/.

93   Karen Hao, "The race to understand the exhilarating, dangerous world of language AI," *MIT Technology Review*, May 20, 2021, https://www .technologyreview.com/2021/05/20/1025135/ai-large-language-models -bigscience-project/.

94   "Are You Overestimating Your Responsible AI Maturity?," BCG, March 30, 2021, https://www.bcg.com/publications/2021/ the-four-stages-of-responsible-ai-maturity.

95   Kai-Fu Lee, *AI Superpowers: China, Silicon Valley, and the New World Order* (Boston: Houghton Mifflin Harcourt, 2018).

96   Lee, *AI Superpowers*, 167.

97   Lee, *AI Superpowers*, 167.

98   Lee, *AI Superpowers*, 185.

Conclusion

99   Ray Kurzweil, "The Law of Accelerating Returns," *Kurzweil: Tracking the acceleration of intelligence* (blog), March 7, 2001, https://www.kurzweilai. net/the-law-of-accelerating-returns.

INDEX

A

accountability, 189, 191, 194

Adobe, 92, 108, 188

adoption of AI, 3–4, 16, 52, 93, 146–147, 173–174, 200–201, 205

advertising and AI
    ad creation, 78–79, 81, 210
    changes in, 76–77
    consumer behavior, 77, 210
    cookies, 77, 81–82, 210–211
    data collection issues, 81–83
    machine learning, 77, 81
    privacy issues, 81–82, 210
    programmatic, 77–78, 81
    RedBalloon example of use of AI, 75–76
    use cases for AI, 78–79
    vendors, 79–81

AI Academy for Marketers, 6–7, 10, 113, 180

AI defined, 1, 12–14, 17, 205

AI in Action, 7

AI Now Institute, 193

AI Score for Marketers, 7, 57–59, 87, 209

AI Superpowers: China, Silicon Valley and the New World Order (Lee), 196

"AI Transformation Playbook" (Ng), 176

AI4ALL, 193

Albert, 75–76, 80

Alexa, 2, 11, 31, 125, 157, 215. *See also* voice assistants

The Algorithmic Leader: How to Be Smart When the Machines Are Smarter Than You (Walsh), 178–179

algorithms
    Amazon, 125, 213
    bias, 185–186. *See also* bias
    defined, 17
    and development of AI, 10, 13
    Google, 43, 151, 215
    and machine learning, 14, 37
    nondisclosure of, 78
    PageRank, 20
    search engines, 150–152, 215
    social media, 165–167, 216

Allen Institute for AI (AI2), 193

Alphabet, 21–23

AlphaGo, 22, 171–173

AlphaGo-The Movie, 172

Altman, Sam, 11

Amazon, 17–19, 77, 109, 122–126, 128, 130, 213

Amazon Web Services (AWS), 17–19, 120, 123, 125, 128, 213

analytics and AI
    adoption of AI, 93

analytics and AI (*continued*)
  Budget Dumpster example, 85–86
  competitive advantage, 88, 211
  cost reduction, 86, 88, 211
  Crayon, 85–86, 89
  large datasets, 86–88, 135, 150, 211
  machine learning, 86–93
  predictive, 86–87, 89
  prescriptive, 87
  revenue growth, 88, 211
  use cases, 87–89
  vendors, 90–93
Anheuser-Busch InBev, 179
Aoun, Joseph E., 180
Apple, 27, 81–82, 185–187
Automate This: How Algorithms Took Over Our Markets, Our Jobs, and Our World (Steiner), 10
Automated Insights, 31–32
automation, intelligent, 3–4, 17, 39–40, 43–45, 48, 51, 56, 59, 64, 121, 165, 191, 195, 197, 199, 208, 218
AutoML, 22, 24
automobile automation, 39–42
avatars, 95–96, 99, 101–102

B

Baidu, 27, 176
barriers to entry, 12, 173–174, 179, 216–217
BCG, 183, 191
BCG GAMMA, 182
BCG Henderson Institute, 182
Bermuda (bot influencer), 101
BERT (bidirectional encoder representations from transformers), 152–153
Bezos, Jeff, 17–18
bias, 33, 52, 165, 175, 185–188, 192, 217
blogs, 6, 31–33, 47, 56, 63, 106, 109–110, 162, 164. *See also* content marketing and AI
bot influencers, 95–96, 99, 101–102

brand, making more human, 183–186. *See also* bias; ethics
brand collateral, 96, 98, 100, 212
Brin, Sergey, 20–23
Budget Dumpster, 85–86
budgets, 70, 78–80, 82, 112, 170
business case for evaluating AI vendors, 48
business goals, 58, 64, 111, 176–177
business listings, 155, 157
Buzzfeed, 103–104

C

call centers, 89, 92
call tracking, 89, 92
Cambridge Analytica, 166
careers, 7, 178, 180–181, 184, 199–201, 204, 217. *See also* jobs, loss of
Carson, Austin, 182
categories of AI, 29, 207. *See also* computer vision; language; prediction
certifications, 180–181
channel management, 14, 89, 119, 170
chatbots, 115–118, 121–122, 124, 178, 213. *See also* conversational agents
Chronicle for Higher Education, 181
churn, 19, 60, 64, 71, 118–119, 129, 141, 144, 170, 215
Clorox, 115–117
Cloud Inference Application Programming Interface (API), 24
cloud services, 16–19, 23, 26–27, 120. *See also* Amazon Web Services (AWS)
Cognitive Content Hub, 110–113
The Cognitive Content Hub: How to Build a More (Artificially) Intelligent Content Engine (online course), 113
communications. *See* public relations, communications, and AI
competitive advantage of AI, 3, 5, 71, 88, 97, 105–106, 174–175, 205, 211
computer vision, 2, 12, 19, 27, 34–36, 127, 161, 207

consumer expectations, 4, 116, 122, 200, 212–213, 218

consumer sentiment, 26, 30, 96, 99, 117–118, 120–121, 127, 153, 163–164, 212–213

Contact Center AI (Google), 120

content marketing and AI

    Buzzfeed, 103–104

    content strategy, 48, 64, 89, 104, 110–113, 156, 212

    cost reduction, 33, 105, 212

    creation of content, 106, 108–110, 212

    The Good Advice Cupcake example, 103–104

    optimizing content, 106–107

    personalization, 106–107, 110

    predicting performance, 107

    recommendations, 106–107

    revenue growth, 105, 109, 212

    skills needed for adapting to use of, 105–106, 212

    use cases for, 104, 106–107

    vendors, 107–110

conversational agents, 117–118, 124, 213. *See also* chatbots

cookies, 77, 81–82, 210–211

CopyAI (copy.ai), 51, 108

cost reduction

    with AI generally, 1, 3, 5, 15, 42, 44, 64, 68–70, 205

    with analytics AI, 86, 88, 211

    as business outcome of AI, 176

    with content marketing AI, 33, 105, 212

    with customer service AI, 118

    with ecommerce AI, 125–126

    pilot projects, 72

    scaling AI, 174

COVID-19, 115–118, 122–124, 166

Crayon, 85–86, 111

Creative Artists Agency (CAA), 95–96

creativity, 3, 34–35, 46, 105, 160, 171–173, 183, 195, 216

crisis communication, 35–36, 101

Cuban, Mark, 16

customer acquisition, 75, 170

customer relationship management (CRM), 49, 56, 60, 87, 108, 119, 121, 135, 140, 145

customer service and AI

    changes in and COVID-19, 115–118, 122, 213

    Clorox smart chatbot example, 115–117

    conversational, 117–118, 120–122, 124, 213. *See also* natural language generation (NLG); natural language processing (NLP)

    cost reduction, 118

    and customer expectations, 116, 122, 212–213

    digital interactions with customers, increase in, 116–117

    insights generated from customer data, 99, 117, 119, 121, 213

    revenue growth, 118

    use cases, 118–119

    vendors, 120–122

customization, 26–27, 37, 107, 131–132, 135–136. *See also* personalization

D

Dali, Salvador, 35

dark side of AI in marketing, 190–191

data

    bias, 33, 52, 165, 175, 186–188, 192, 217

    inputs, 36, 44–46, 51, 207–209

    and machine learning, 207

    training data, 18, 41, 52, 171, 186–187

    visualization tool, 170

data collection issues, 81–83, 175

data flywheel, 82–83, 125

data strategy, 174–175

databases, 97, 119, 130, 133–136, 145, 214

datasets, 86–88, 135, 150, 211. *See also* analytics and AI

Dean, Jeff, 24

deep learning, 2, 12, 14–17, 22, 25, 32,
43, 50, 56, 120, 169, 172, 177, 181, 201,
205–206
deepfakes, 35–36, 101–102
DeepMind, 1, 22, 171–172
demand forecasting, 126
dependence, 46, 209
Descript, 63, 108–109
discovery phase of problem-based model,
66–68
Drift, 120, 139–140, 144
Dynamics 365, 121

E

ecommerce and AI
advantages of buying versus building
AI system, 130
Amazon, 123–125, 128, 213
conversational agents, 118, 124, 213
cost reduction, 125–126
and COVID-19 pandemic, 123–124
Pomelo Fashion example, 123–124,
130
return on investment (ROI), 124, 130
revenue growth from, 125
use cases for, 125–127
vendors, 128–130
efficiency, 5, 29, 48, 51, 69, 72, 126, 173, 175,
190, 195, 207
email marketing and AI
issues with, 137
Moscona, Matt, example, 131–132
personalization, 37–38
segmented lists, 132, 135–137, 214
subject lines, 13, 37, 43, 107, 109,
132–134, 136, 175, 214
use cases for, 133–135
value of, 132–133, 214
vendors, 135–136
emotion detection, 27, 34, 118, 164
empathy, 3, 117, 122, 183, 195, 199, 213
enterprise resource planning (ERP), 121

ethics, 49–50, 52, 69, 167, 179, 183, 186–
190, 192, 217

F

Facebook, 2, 11, 76–78, 80, 92, 109–110,
166. See also Meta
facial recognition, 2, 27, 34, 207
fears concerning AI, 5, 12, 71, 147, 200
Federated Learning of Cohorts (FLoC), 82
Festetics, Tassilo, 179
5 Ps of marketing AI, 57–62, 209
forecasting, 18, 36, 124, 126, 133, 141–142,
213
Frase, 109, 111
Friedman, Adam, 95
fulfillment centers, 125–126
future of AI, 1–3, 5, 197, 199–200, 203–205

G

GaryVee TV, 160
Gates, Bill, 25
Gebru, Timmit, 189
Glover, Joseph, 181
Gmail, 2, 11, 23, 43
Goldman Sachs, 185
The Good Advice Cupcake, 103–104
Goodby, Silverstein & Partners (GS&P), 35
Google, 2, 20–24, 43, 77, 81–82, 149, 151–
153, 180, 188–189, 194, 215
Google Ads, 23, 109
Google Analytics, 23, 86, 88, 91, 93
Google Assistant, 23, 31, 120
Google Brain team, 176
Google China, 196
Google Cloud, 18, 23, 120
Google Docs, 23
Google Home, 21
Google Maps, 23
Google Search, 23
Google Sheets, 23
Google Smart Compose, 43
Google Translate, 21, 23
Google Trends, 110

GPT, 32
GPT-2, 32–33
GPT-3, 33, 51, 98, 106, 108
Grow Smarter with AI, 6

H
Hansson, David Heinemeier, 185–186
Hao, Karen, 189
harmful applications of AI, 189–190. *See also* deepfakes; ethics
Hassabis, Demis, 1, 12
higher education, 180–182, 199–200
Hoffman, Reid, 32
HubSpot, 10, 145, 156
humans and machines
    and creativity. *See* creativity
    distinguished, 196–197
    future of, 203–204
    human-centered AI, 183, 192–197
    Marketer-to-Machine (M2M) Scale, 43–46, 51, 54, 175, 208
    mutual learning, 182–183
    relationship between, 1–2, 13, 199

I
IBM, 27, 115
image recognition, 15, 27, 34, 127, 161, 206–207, 216
improvement, 46, 209
influencers, 92, 95–97, 99, 101–102
inputs, 13, 36, 44–46, 51, 207–209. *See also* data; training data
insights
    analytics, 85–92, 211
    customer service, 117, 119, 121, 213
    public relations, 97, 99, 101, 211
    sales, 139, 141, 214
    SEO, 152, 154, 156, 215
    social media marketing, 162–164
Instagram, 95, 101, 103, 109
Institute for Human-Centered AI (HAI), 193–194

integration of AI technology, 47, 49, 53, 69–71, 195
intelligent automation. *See* automation, intelligent
intent, in searches, 150, 153–154, 156, 215
Internet of Things, 26, 170, 216
inventory management, 126

J
Jasper, 51, 109
jobs, loss of, 12, 33, 139, 184, 196, 199, 201, 217. *See also* careers

K
Kahn, Jeremy, 166
Kaput, Mike, 6, 8
key performance indicators (KPIs), 44, 67, 79–80, 93, 111
Khodabandeh, Shervin, 183
Kurzweil, Ray, 203–204

L
language
    Amazon solutions, 17–19
    applications, 30–31
    content creation. *See* content marketing and AI
    Google solutions, 23. *See also* Google
    Microsoft solutions, 26–27
    natural language generation. *See* natural language generation (NLG)
    natural language processing. *See* natural language processing (NLP)
    sentiment analysis. *See* sentiment analysis and detection
    speaker identification, 27, 30–31
    speech to text, 19, 23, 26, 30
    text to speech, 30, 108
    translation, 15, 19, 21, 23, 26–27, 30, 206
    voice assistants. *See* voice assistants
large language models (LLMs), 189

Lately, 159, 164

leadership, educating and engaging, 70, 177

leads, scoring and qualifying, 52, 59, 87–88, 134, 139–143, 145–146

Lee, Kai-Fu, 196

Lil Miquela, 95–96, 99, 101

LinkedIn, 7, 9

Linkfluence, 101, 164–165

Lyu, Siwei, 36

M

machine learning
    advertising, 77, 81
    AI technology, 2, 13–14, 31, 205
    algorithms. *See* algorithms
    Amazon Web Services (AWS), 18–19, 125
    analytics, 86–93
    and data, 207
    deep learning. *See* deep learning
    defined, 17
    described, 13–14, 206
    ecommerce AI, 128–129
    Google, 21–23, 91
    improvement, 46, 209
    and prediction, 36, 51–52, 207. *See also* prediction
    and programmatic advertising, 77
    Tesla, 40–41, 46
    value of for global economy, 169
    and vendor assessments, 47, 50–52

MAICON (Marketing AI Conference), 6–7, 10, 195

Malachowsky, Chris, 181

Marketer-to-Machine (M2M) Scale, 43–46, 51, 54, 175, 208

The Marketing Agency Blueprint (Roetzer), 10

marketing AI, defined, 17, 205

marketing AI, framework for getting started with
    development of, 55–56

5 Ps, 56–62, 209–210
    frequently asked questions, 71–73
    pilot projects, 64–65, 71–73, 210
    problem-based model, 66–71
    use cases, identifying and prioritizing, 63–65
    use cases, tool for rating, 57–63, 209–210

Marketing AI Conference (MAICON), 6–7, 10, 195

Marketing AI Institute, 6–7, 42–43, 56, 110, 180, 199

Marketing AI Show (podcast), 6

Marketing Artificial Intelligence Institute, 10

marketing team, 53–54, 71, 174, 177–180

MarketMuse, 109–111, 149–150, 156–157

Martin, Cheryl, 181

McKinsey Global Institute, 169–171, 173

Meta, 27, 77–78, 82. *See also* Facebook

metrics for evaluating AI, 72, 93, 177

Metz, Cade, 172

Microsoft, 25–27, 180

Microsoft Dynamics 365, 121

MIT Sloan Management Review, 182

Mitchell, Margaret, 189

Monday.com, 149–150

Moscona, Matt, 131–132

Mossberg, Walt, 17–18

movement detection, 34

MQL (marketing qualfied lead), 139–140, 142

MUM (multitask unified model), 153

Musk, Elon, 32

N

Nadella, Satya, 25

natural language generation (NLG), 2, 12, 30–33, 47, 50–52, 79, 81, 98, 106, 108–109, 118, 134, 162. *See also* voice assistants

natural language processing (NLP), 2, 12, 18–19, 23–24, 30–31, 79, 81, 115–118, 122, 128–130, 134, 162
natural language understanding (NLU), 121
neural nets, 15
neural networks, 10, 12, 21–22, 41–42, 120, 201
Nevill-Spencer, Dudley, 96
Ng, Andrew, 175–176
NLG. *See* natural language generation (NLG)
NLP. *See* natural language processing (NLP)
NVIDIA, 27, 181–182

O

obsolescence, 33, 49, 178, 204
Okta, 139–140
OpenAI, 11, 32–33
overhyping of technology, 47, 52, 55–56
oversight, 45–46, 209

P

Page, Larry, 20–21, 23
Pardes, Arielle, 177
Partnership on AI (PAI), 194
pattern recognition, 13, 36, 86, 88, 126, 133, 135, 141, 154, 162, 211, 214–215
Pattern89, 45, 80–81
performance, maximizing, 5, 13–14, 29, 51, 79, 107, 207. *See also* 5 Ps of marketing AI; key performance indicators (KPIs)
personalization, 2–3, 19, 26, 36–38, 57–58, 61, 67, 126, 128, 130, 132, 186, 190–191, 195, 197, 205, 209, 217–218
Pichai, Sundar, 22–23
pilot projects, 64–73, 175–177, 210
Piloting AI Workbook, 65
planning phase of problem-based model, 66, 69–71
Pomelo Fashion, 123–124, 130
PR 20/20, 6, 10, 31, 179

Pragmatic Digital, 158
prediction. *See also* insights
  advertising, 79
  AI technology, 1, 207
  applications of, 36
  benefits of for marketers, 1, 13–14
  churn, 118–119
  forecasting, 18, 36
  inputs. *See* inputs
  and machine learning, 13–14, 36, 51–52, 207
  pattern recognition. *See* pattern recognition
  personalization. *See* personalization
  power of in marketing, 37–38
  for product development, 127
  recommendation, 36
Prediction Machines: The Simple Economics off Artificial Intelligence (Agrawal, Gans, and Goldfarb), 36–37
predictive keyword research, 154
press releases, 32–33, 97–98
pricing, 127, 169–170, 176
privacy issues, 81–83, 175, 183–184, 191–192, 218
problem-based model for pilot project, 66–70, 210
product searches, 127
productivity, 5, 37, 141, 143
Project Copyscale, 31–32
prospects, 134, 139–142, 144, 146–147
public relations, communications, and AI
  brand perceptions, shaping, 96–98, 211–212
  competitive advantage of AI, 97
  crisis communication, 35–36, 101
  deepfakes, 101–102
  Lil Miquela example, 95–96, 99, 101
  relationship building, 96–97
  use cases, 98–99
  vendors, 99–101

R

Ransbotham, Sam, 182
RedBalloon, 75–76
Redmond, Michael, 172
relationship building, 183, 195
reputation, 98, 101, 157
responsible practices, 191–194, 197, 217–218
return on investment (ROI), 3, 13, 62, 70, 76, 124, 130, 176
revenue growth
    with AI generally, 1, 3, 5, 15, 42, 44, 64, 68, 205
    with analytics AI, 88, 211
    as business outcome of AI, 176
    with content marketing AI, 105, 109, 212
    with customer service AI, 118
    with ecommerce AI, 125
    and pilot projects, 72–73
    with scaling AI, 174
robotics, 19, 24, 125–126
Robot-Proof: Higher Education in the Age of Artificial Intelligence (Aoun), 180
Roetzer, Paul, 8
ROI (return on investment), 3, 13, 62, 70, 124, 130, 176

S

sales and AI
    adopting, steps for enabling sales team, 146–147
    benefits of, 140–141, 214–215
    leads, scoring and qualifying, 52, 59, 87–88, 134, 139–143, 145–146
    Okta example using Drift, 139–140
    use cases for, 141–143
    vendors, 144–146
sales cycle, shortening, 4, 177
Salesforce, 27, 141, 145–146
Salesforce Futures Lab, 82
scaling and AI
    and creativity, 171–173, 216
    financial impact of AI, 169–170, 216
    framework for, 173–184
    industries, 169–170
    job loss and career opportunities, 179–181, 184, 217. *See also* careers; jobs, loss of
search engine optimization (SEO). *See* SEO and AI
search engines, 20
security and compliance, 24, 50, 69, 175, 192
Sedol, Lee, 22, 171–173
sentiment analysis and detection, 26, 30, 96, 99, 117–118, 120–121, 127, 153, 163–164, 212–213
SEO and AI
    Google technology developments, 152–153, 215
    importance of, 151–152, 215
    Monday.com example using MarketMuse, 149–150
    pattern recognition, 154, 215. *See also* pattern recognition
    use cases for, 154–155
    vendors, 155–157
    voice search, 151, 155–158, 215
Shipley, Nathan, 35
Silver, David, 172
Simson, Naomi, 75–76
Siri, 2, 31, 157, 215. *See also* voice assistants
social media marketing and AI
    benefits of, 160–161, 216
    manipulative messaging, 165–167, 216–217
    market growth, 161
    use cases for, 161–163
    VaynerMedia example using Lately, 159–160
    vendors, 163–165
software as a service (SaaS), 92, 152
speech to text technology, 19, 23, 26, 30
SQL (sales qualified lead), 140

Stanford Institute for Human-Centered
    Artificial Intelligence (HAI), 193–194
Steiner, Christopher, 10
Stitch Fix, 177–178
structured data, 23–24, 45, 68, 209
Sweezey, Mathew, 82

T
2021 State of Marketing AI Report, 12,
    58–63, 65, 104, 173, 179
Talkwalker, 34, 101
technology, rapid changes in, 11, 199–200,
    203–204, 218
technology companies, major, 27. *See also*
    specific companies
terminology, 16–17, 30
Tesla, 39–42, 45–46
text-to-speech technology, 23, 26, 30, 108
Thiel, Peter, 32
time to value (TTV), 54, 175
training and onboarding, 5, 12, 45, 49,
    52–54, 70–71, 118, 179–180, 208–209
training data, 15, 18, 41, 52, 171, 186–187
translation, 15, 19, 21, 23, 26–27, 30, 206
transparency, 192, 194
Trump, Donald, 166
Twitter, 24, 160, 165–166

U
understanding of AI, need for, 178, 201,
    204, 218
University of Florida, 181–182
unstructured data, 13, 26, 45, 68, 209
use cases
    for advertising AI, 78–79
    for analytics AI, 87–89
    for content marketing AI, 106–107
    for customer service AI, 118–119
    for ecommerce AI, 125–127
    for email marketing AI, 133–135
    for evaluating AI technology and
        vendors, 50–51, 57–65

5 Ps framework for identifying,
    56–63, 209–210
Piloting AI Workbook for identifying
    and prioritizing, 65
prioritizing, 65, 175–176
for public relations and
    communications AI, 98–99
for sales AI, 141–143
for SEO AI, 154–155
for social media AI, 161–163
subjective nature of, 63, 209
top ten for marketing AI, 62–63

V
Vaynerchuk, Gary, 159–160
VaynerMedia, 159–160
vendors
    advertising AI, 79–81
    analytics AI, 90–93
    assessment tool, 58
    business case for evaluating, 48
    content marketing AI, 107–110
    customer service AI, 120–122
    ecommerce AI, 128–130
    email marketing AI, 135–136
    evaluating, 47–54, 57–65
    product maturity levels, 47
    profiles of, 47, 56
    public relations, communications,
        and AI, 99–101
    sales AI, 144–146
    SEO AI, 155–157
    social media marketing AI, 163–165
    use cases for evaluating AI
        technology and vendors, 50–51,
        57–65
video recognition, 34, 207
videos, 35–36, 108
virtual agents, 23, 118, 120–121. *See also*
    customer service and AI
virtual try-on, 126–127
vision. *See* computer vision

voice assistants, 2, 11, 15, 31, 125, 155,
    157–158, 170, 184, 206, 215–216. *See also*
    SEO and AI

W

Walsh, Mike, 178–179
Watson (IBM), 10
Westwater, Scot, 158
Westwater, Susan, 158
Women in AI (WAI), 194
World Wide Web, 20
Wozniak, Steve, 185

Y

YouTube, 21, 23, 36, 166

Z

Zuckerberg, Mark, 166

ABOUT THE AUTHORS

Paul Roetzer is founder and CEO of Marketing AI Institute and PR 20/20; author of *The Marketing Performance Blueprint* (Wiley, 2014), and *The Marketing Agency Blueprint* (Wiley, 2012); and creator of the Marketing Artificial Intelligence Conference (MAICON). As a speaker, Roetzer is focused on making AI approachable and actionable for marketers and business leaders. A graduate of Ohio University's E.W. Scripps School of Journalism, Roetzer has consulted for hundreds of organizations, from startups to Fortune 500 companies.

Mike Kaput is the chief content officer at Marketing AI Institute. Kaput uses content marketing, marketing strategy, and marketing technology to grow and scale traffic, leads, and revenue for Marketing AI Institute. An avid writer, Mike has published hundreds of articles on how to use AI in marketing to increase revenue and reduce costs. He is also the author of *Bitcoin in Plain English*, a beginner's guide to the world's most popular cryptocurrency.